today i will

EILEEN & JERRY SPINELLI

today i will

A YEAR *of* QUOTES, NOTES,
and PROMISES *to* MYSELF

illustrated by
Julia Rothman

Alfred A. Knopf

New York

THIS IS A BORZOI BOOK PUBLISHED BY ALFRED A. KNOPF

Text copyright © 2009 by Eileen Spinelli and Jerry Spinelli
Illustrations copyright © 2009 by Julia Rothman

Visit us on the Web! www.randomhouse.com/kids

Educators and librarians, for a variety of teaching tools, visit us at
www.randomhouse.com/teachers

Library of Congress Cataloging-in-Publication Data
Spinelli, Eileen.
Today I will : a year of quotes, notes, and promises to myself / Eileen and Jerry Spinelli ;
with illustrations by Julia Rothman. — 1st ed.
    p. cm.
"This is a Borzoi book."
ISBN 978-0-375-84057-9 (trade) — ISBN 978-0-375-96230-1 (lib. bdg.)
1. Conduct of life—Quotations, maxims, etc.—Juvenile literature. 2. Children's
literature—Quotations, maxims, etc.—Juvenile literature. I. Spinelli, Jerry. II. Title.
PN6084.C556S74 2009
082—dc22
2008047869

Printed in the United States of America
October 2009
10 9 8 7 6 5 4 3 2 1

First Edition

To

Bruce and Dee Lindeman

and

Greg and Cindy Peterson

"A happy New Year to all the world!"

—*A Christmas Carol*
by Charles Dickens

A year of time lies ahead of us. Who knows the countless things, big and small, that will happen? Much will be out of our control. As for now, at the start of another lap around our star, let's just drop all distinctions for the moment and simply wish the best for all of us, passengers together on this ship called Earth.

Today I will play no favorites. I will wish
the whole world a "Happy New Year!"

You never know when something begins where it's going to take you.

—*A Gathering of Days:
A New England Girl's Journal, 1830–32*
by Joan W. Blos

And isn't that precisely what makes life an adventure? Imagine starting out the year today—OK, yesterday—and knowing exactly where you'll be on December 31st. A year without surprises, without twists and turns, without suspense. It would be like the most boring story you ever read.

Today I will welcome surprises.

There's something about a blank page that makes me tingle.

—*Jazmin's Notebook*
by Nikki Grimes

You can take those words—*a blank page*—literally, or you can take them to mean any aspect of your life that is empty, a blank space. We all have blank pages in our lives: a thank-you or an apology not yet expressed, a forgiveness not yet offered, a challenge not yet attempted, a vegetable not yet tasted. Do the blank pages in your life make you tingle? Or retreat?

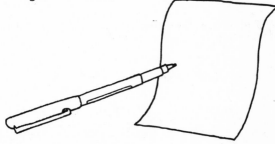

There's a stack of blank pages in my life. Some of them, frankly, don't exactly excite me. But others do. Today I'll pick one out and fill it in.

S mall steps,
'Cause I don't know where I'm goin'.

—*Small Steps*
by Louis Sachar

If you don't know where you're going, it's important to admit it to yourself and act accordingly. This applies whether you're trying to find your way out of a carnival fun house or into your own future. Do you want to try out for the school play? Get a part-time job? Go to college? Get a tattoo? Each question has at least two answers. They're waiting along the road ahead of you. Take small steps, lest you blow by the best one.

I know I'm on my way, but darned if I know where. That's why I'm going to take it small step by small step. Doing so will allow me to avoid pitfalls and change direction, helping ensure that I wind up exactly where I want to be.

Auntie lived down the road a piece.

—*Epossumondas Saves the Day*
by Coleen Salley
illustrated by Janet Stevens

Aunties—and uncles and cousins and grandparents—don't always live just down the road. Sometimes they live in the next state or across the country or on the other side of the world. Don't let distance be an excuse for ignoring favorite relatives. Write to them. E-mail them. Call them. Once you reach out, everybody is just "down the road a piece."

I have a couple of favorite relatives, but because they're so far away, I tend to ignore them—even though they have mailboxes, e-mail addresses, and telephone numbers. Today, I'll get back in touch.

"What's up, Louie?
Why so sad?"
Barney asked.
"The kids are laughin' at me."

—*Regards to the Man in the Moon*
by Ezra Jack Keats

HAHAHA

Isn't it ironic that two opposite expressions—laughter and sadness—often go together? Ironic maybe, but no surprise to anyone who's ever been mocked and ridiculed. Unless you can honestly say that being mocked never bothers you, you have no right to mock others. In fact, even if you enjoy being mocked, you still have no right.

Sometimes I pretend that I don't sense the feelings of others—but, really, I do. I understand that ridicule hurts feelings. I understand that I should treat others as I want to be treated. Bottom line: From this day forward, I am a Mock-Not Zone.

"**M**arty, don't you *ever* run away
from a problem."

—Shiloh
by Phyllis Reynolds Naylor

It's OK to *want* to run away from a problem. That's human nature. Little kids do it all the time, and it's allowed because, well, they're little. But whether you're five or fifteen, the day you face a problem and run *toward* it rather than *away* from it—that's the day the grown-up you is born.

Before this day is over, I'll probably face at least one
problem I want to run away from. But I won't.

*H*unger is a pretty terrible thing.
It's like going around all day with a nail
in your shoe. You try to put it out
of your mind, but you never really
quite forget it.

—*My Brother Sam Is Dead*
by James Lincoln Collier and Christopher Collier

Have you ever been *really* hungry? Not I'm-an-hour-late-for-dinner hungry, but I-haven't-eaten-since-two-days-ago hungry? You probably haven't. But many people have. Many people are hungry even now, as you're heading for breakfast. Maybe you should remember this next time you're about to say "I'm starving!" Maybe you should think about it. Maybe you should do something.

Do I have $5 to spare? Today I'll ask my parents how I can donate it to help feed a really hungry person. And—unless it's true—I'll never again say "I'm starving!"

Dawn was sitting on her front steps. She was reading a fat book.

—*Pickle Puss*
by Patricia Reilly Giff
illustrated by Blanche Sims

When you're assigned to read a book, do you stand there scanning the library shelves, making it look as if you're searching for the best title when what you're really doing is looking for the skinniest one?

Is that the way I go about book-looking? The thinner the better? Avoid fat books like a gym class dodge ball? What am I afraid of—having too much fun?

"The zoo is kid stuff," Miguel tells
his sister.
"I am a kid!" Juanita states. "And
you're a kid, too."

—*How Tía Lola Came to ~~Visit~~ Stay*
by Julia Alvarez

Of all the mistakes that kids make, this may be the most common: They don't enjoy being a kid. Starting with every birthday, we join a new club—the Eleven-Year-Old Club, the Twelve-Year-Old Club, etc. We belong for 365 days, and then we're out. We could live to 1,000, but we'll never belong to that particular club again. If we're smart, we'll enjoy where and when we are and not keep itching forward to the next year.

I'll be happy with the club I'm in today and not gripe about what I'm not yet allowed to do.

"It's okay to cry when someone you like very much has died."

—*I Remember Miss Perry*
by Pat Brisson
illustrated by Stéphane Jorisch

This page, like most of these pages, is for everybody—but it's especially for guys who think it's unmanly or uncool to cry. News flash: Real men *do* cry. And cool is only a few degrees south of cold. You were born with tear ducts— use them.

OK—I still won't be a big baby and start bawling over every little thing, but neither will I dishonor my humanity by staying stubbornly cool when my feelings cry out for tears.

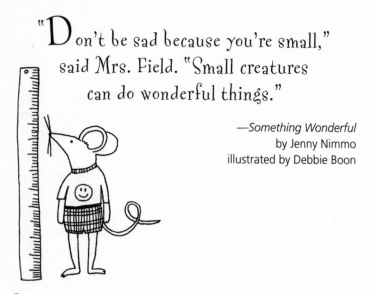

"Don't be sad because you're small," said Mrs. Field. "Small creatures can do wonderful things."

—*Something Wonderful*
by Jenny Nimmo
illustrated by Debbie Boon

Size is overrated, as any dog infested with fleas can tell you. So take note. This applies to you whether you are small (no problem, you can still do it) or big (don't think your size is all you need).

Have I been assuming that I have an edge because I'm big—
or a curse because I'm small? If so, today I'll scrap
that junk and replace it with this:

Do I really want the prize?
Gumption gets it, not my size.

"Look. Somebody's going to be
worried about you."

—*The Great Gilly Hopkins*
by Katherine Paterson

People care about you, worry about you. You may think it's a pain, but in fact it's a wonderful compliment to you and one of the greatest gifts you'll ever get. Don't spurn it. Cherish it. If you ever become so unlucky that nobody worries about you, you'll desperately wish someone would.

Sometimes my parents' constant worry about me
feels more like a hassle than a gift, but even if I can't
always see it their way, I'll respect them enough
to let them know where I am and to come home on time.

"Silence can be a good thing, you know, partly because it helps one to listen."

—*Clair de Lune*
by Cassandra Golds
illustrated by Sophie Blackall

We're talkers, we humans. We love to talk. We love to hear ourselves. How much we miss because our ears are filled with the sound of our own voices!

Today I will enrich my life: I will shut my mouth. I will make no noise. I will pursue silence. I will . . . *listen.*

I've always been a dreamer.

—*My Dream of Martin Luther King*
by Faith Ringgold

There is almost nothing good in this world that did not begin as a dream in someone's head. Of course, dreaming alone isn't enough. The dream must be incubated, hatched, nourished, and guided to maturity. But in the beginning there is that essential seed. In the beginning is the dream.

Yes, I will be a doer, a worker, an improver. But to begin with, I will be a dreamer. I will give my dreams a room of their own, where they can romp and play and develop until one of them is ready for action.

There's a lot of pressure on kids to excel both in class and on the playing field.

—"In Defense of Misfits"
by Andrea Uva
(from *The Courage to Be Yourself:
True Stories by Teens About Cliques,
Conflicts, and Overcoming Peer Pressure*,
edited by Al Desetta, M.A., with Educators for Social Responsibility)

Does this describe your situation? If you're feeling pressure from parents, coaches, teachers, friends, whoever, it's useless for this book to tell you "Don't sweat it. Just ignore the pressure." Because that's the problem—you *can't* ignore it. Since the pressure won't go away, your best bet is to learn to live with it—meaning carve out stress-free pockets for yourself. At least once a day do something just for the fun of it. Goof off. Laugh. Lose. Come in last. Who cares?!

I won't be pressured into high achievement every minute of my life. I will reserve minutes today and every day from now on just for fun, just for me.

So it turned out I was okay at some things but really awful at others.

—*The Off Season*
by Catherine Gilbert Murdock

Is there something you really stink at? Come on, admit it—
it's just between you and this page. Is it singing? dancing?
sports? spelling? darts? remembering to flush the toilet?
In fact, if you had to make a list of Stuff I Stink At, you
could probably list ten things without your brain breaking
a sweat. Now, some of these I-stink-at things might be
worth your while to work on and get better at. But others—
why bother? Because nobody is good at everything—
nobody—and it's important to know that you'll never
become comfortable with yourself until you come to terms
with your minuses as well as your pluses.

OK, I admit it (to this page, anyway)—I'm not perfect.
Sometimes I see kids do stuff that I know I'll never be able to do
as well. And that's cool. I'm OK with it. For three reasons:
(1) It's all part of who I am. (2) Who cares how good I am as
long as I enjoy it? (3) Nobody else is perfect either.

"But which one is the best?" asked Emily. "Whichever one *you* like," her mother replied.

—*Emily's Art*
by Peter Catalanotto

Tired of being told what's "best for you"? If so, you'll be happy to know that what you want and what is "best" are sometimes the same thing. This is most commonly true in matters of personal taste. If you are the only kid in your school whose favorite color is puce, or who loves asparagus, or who's crazy about zither music, who's to tell you you're wrong?

My own personal tastes are just that—mine.
Hey, I like what I like. End of story.

It was late one winter night,
long past my bedtime,
when Pa and I went owling.

—*Owl Moon*
by Jane Yolen
illustrated by John Schoenherr

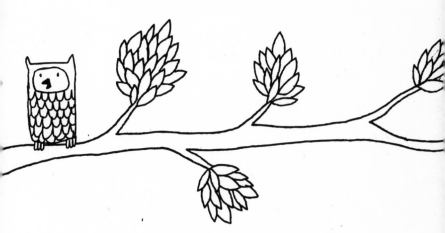

Have you ever gone owling? Have you ever stood still on a winter's night and heard the call of an unseen owl? If not, you're missing something.

Tonight, or some night soon, I will go owling.

"This hawk was hit by a car, and its wing was injured," said Hannah. "The driver brought him here."

—*In Good Hands: Behind the Scenes at a Center for Orphaned and Injured Birds* by Stephen R. Swinburne

Accidents don't happen only on the highway. Example: You accidentally break a neighbor's window. Do you pretend you know nothing about it? Or do you confess and offer to pay for it? Example: You say to a friend, "The burgers at lunch today stank"—only to discover that a lunchroom lady is walking behind you. Do you breeze along on your way—or try to make amends ("But the fries were great!")?

Accidents happen to everybody. What matters is how I respond. I will not be a hit-and-runner; I'll be a hit-and-helper.

If more of us valued food and cheer and song above hoarded gold, it would be a merrier world.

—*The Hobbit*
by J.R.R. Tolkien

Do you check out your friends' labels and know instantly what they paid for their clothes? Do you and your friends brag about how much your holiday and birthday gifts cost your parents? Could you name everyone in your class who is richer than you? poorer than you? Do you, maybe, perhaps, look down your nose just a teensy little bit at the poorer ones?

How much does money matter to me?
More than cheer and song? Do I have my values in order?
Today I'll take stock.

Each of us should be able at least to "brighten the corner" where we are.

—*Charlie Brown, Snoopy and Me*
by Charles M. Schulz

If you come to the end of your road and you can't say you've done that, what's the point?

Today I'll do something that makes my corner of this world just a little brighter.

*H*e loved the Hudson City YMCA,
where he'd become hooked on athletics
during a season of indoor floor hockey
as a first-grader.

—*Emergency Quarterback*
by Rich Wallace

When you think of a dominant institution in your life, you probably think of school. But look around. You are surrounded by opportunities to participate, to belong, to learn from. The Y. Dance academy. Library. Local theater. Boys & Girls Clubs. Scouts. Church. Book club. Martial arts. Volunteer activities . . . Well, you get the point.

Am I taking advantage of what my community has to offer?
Am I ignoring opportunities to get hooked on a lifelong
passion? The bait is here, dangling all around me.
Today I'll bite.

O h, Callie—I miss you so!

—*Mama, Let's Dance*
by Patricia Hermes

If you had to express the human experience in just six words, the quote above would be as good a choice as any. In this heartfelt cry, we hear the love, the good and bad times, the shared history of two human beings, two earthlings. The experience doesn't end with the exit of one person or pet but rather continues in the heart and outcry of the one left behind. No book, not this one or any other, can duplicate the experience or erase the pain. In crying out, you are being as human as you can be.

There is no specific instruction for today. Simply this: a heartening confirmation that my relationships with others are the most and the best of my earthly experience. And a reminder that the time I share with my family and friends is something to be celebrated and lived to the fullest.

"I thought I was invisible before you."

—*The Opposite of Invisible*
by Liz Gallagher

This is what Alice says to Simon as she breaks up with him. Lots of kids are like Alice. They think that until some special person sees them, nobody does. Not even themselves. Their self-esteem is so low, they're surprised when an automatic supermarket door opens for them.

Am I visible to others? More important, am I visible to myself? Do I get down on myself? Do I think I'm worthless? Do I think if I disappeared tomorrow, the world wouldn't even notice? Here's the thing: If I'm visible to myself—if I am worthy in my own eyes—then I will surely be visible to others.

For me, reading books and writing them are tied together. The words of other writers teach me and refresh me and inspire me.

—*The Moon and I*
by Betsy Byars

Stuck on a writing assignment? Need an idea? a kick start? You're in luck. You've just been reminded that writing and reading are related. They feed off each other. You are reaching for a book . . . reaching for a book. . . .

I hate it: the dreaded Writer's Block. Brain Constipation. Next time it hits me, I'll be smart. I'll seek help. I'll remember that writing's sibling is reading. Right over there is a book I've enjoyed before. I'll reach for it. . . .

Then yesterday, before my bath,
As I took off my clothes,
A chunk of something gray and wet
Fell right out of my nose.

—*Parts*
by Tedd Arnold

The boy in the book is a hypochondriac. He's always imagining that things are wrong with him. He doesn't enjoy his own good health because he's so worried about every little twitch and bump.

Is there a hypochondriac in me? If so, I'm going to show it the door. Hypo, you're not coming between me and my good health!

My friends thought I was crazy.

—*Brave Harriet: The First Woman to Fly the English Channel*
(biography of Harriet Quimby)
by Marissa Moss
illustrated by C. F. Payne

Do your friends ever think you're crazy? If not, check yourself—you may be in danger of becoming boring. Surprise your friends. Surprise *yourself*.

Today I'll do something unpredictable.

And nobody did or said anything to make me feel like I didn't belong.

—*In the Wild*
by Sofia Nordin
translated by Maria Lundin

It's not always that way, is it? A turn of the shoulder. A tone of voice. A silent phone. An empty mailbox. A closed door. Belongers are very good at letting others know they're not welcome. Remember this: Belonging is something *you* decide, not *them*. You are worthy. You have standing in this world. Maybe they just don't see it—yet.

Do I feel unwelcome somewhere? Well, I have news for them. The universe—you can't get bigger than that!—welcomes me into the Humanhood of Life, the Society of All Creatures. I *do* belong.

Franklin knew how to entertain himself.

—*Make Your Mark, Franklin Roosevelt*
by Judith St. George
illustrated by Britt Spencer

Back in the 1900s, a kid entertained himself or herself by bouncing a ball against a wall, riding a bike, reading a book. These days it's video games and handheld electronics—and still, we hope, books. While the companionship of others is important, even essential, to a kid's life, so is the ability to go it alone, to provide your own entertainment. You are heading for independence. You are an apprentice adult. This is part of your training.

If I find myself alone today, will I feel lost? empty? helpless? Will I feel my life can't go on until I'm in the company of my friends? Am I such poor company to myself? I hope not.

JANUARY 31
(JACKIE ROBINSON'S BIRTHDAY)

In some cities Robinson is not allowed to stay in the same hotels or eat in the same restaurants as his white teammates.

—Baseball's Best: Five True Stories
by Andrew Gutelle
illustrated by Cliff Spohn

By the time Jackie Robinson retired from baseball, every team in the major leagues was integrated and players of all colors shared hotels and restaurants. History credits Robinson with breaking the so-called color line in baseball. More than half a century later, many other lines remain—lines that separate the rich from the not-rich, the beautiful from the not-beautiful, the jocks from the eggheads, the Goths from the preppies, the able from the challenged. History awaits more Jackie Robinsons.

Lines of separation are all around me. Do I follow these lines? Or do I dare to be a pioneer, dare to break them?

It is also human nature to define
a person by his or her job,
which is a mistake.

—*The Sledding Hill*
by Chris Crutcher

In many cases, a big mistake. When you know a person's job, you know only what that person *does* for a living, not who that person *is*.

I already think about what my life's work might be, my job.
But that will never be the total me. I will always be more
than my job. No matter how much I love my job,
I will never allow it to become all of me.
And I will keep this in mind when I consider others.

"What about the consequences?"

—*Catalyst*
by Laurie Halse Anderson

Consequences? You mean, like, I can't do bad stuff and get away with it? You mean if I break the law—whether it's parents' or police law—there's a price to pay? You mean the stupid, inconsiderate, foolish decision I make today could bite me in the rump tomorrow?

I understand that the answer to all the above is: Yes.
I understand that there's a connection between what I do
today and what happens tomorrow—or even for the rest
of my life. So I'll make today's decision a good one.

*H*ome is more than just the place
we return to after being away.

—*Home: A Journey through America*
paintings by Thomas Locker
compiled and edited by Candace Christiansen

True enough. And here's the rest of it: You may never understand all that your home means to you *until* you leave it. Don't like your home? Wait till you leave it for a while. Don't be surprised if you miss it.

Today I will list five things I love about my home,
things that I would miss if I were away.

She [Rosa Parks] was not going to give in to that which was wrong.

—*Rosa*
by Nikki Giovanni
illustrated by Bryan Collier

Doing the wrong thing wouldn't be so common if it weren't for this: Doing the wrong thing is often easier than doing the right thing. Think about it. If only nature would arrange it so that doing the wrong thing was really, really a pain—who would take the trouble? But in this real world, life doesn't seem to work that way. In fact, in many cases, all the wrong thing requires of you is that you do . . . nothing. Nothing at all. Just give in.

Do I tend to take the easy way out? Do I decide what to do based on right/wrong? or hard/easy? Do I understand that sometimes doing nothing is actually doing wrong? Do I give in—or dig in? Today, just for myself, I'll seek honest answers to these questions.

Get plenty of sleep, and stop worrying.

—*Charlotte's Web*
by E. B. White

You've been around the block a time or two. And you've learned what five-year-olds haven't yet: Life isn't always pretty and easy and fun. And sometimes there's not a dog-gone thing you can do about it. You've tried worrying yourself silly. You've tried losing sleep. Doesn't work, does it? Well, maybe you can learn something from those little kids after all. Think about it—have you ever seen a sleepless five-year-old worrywart?

I'll live today to the max. Then sleep
the Sleep of No Worries tonight.

"You'll know this for yourself, someday,"
Ellie said. "How forgiveness
sets you free."

—*Tell Me Everything*
by Carolyn Coman

Are you harboring a hatred? Or, more to the point, is a hatred harboring you? Did someone do something bad to you? say something bad about you? something you can't forgive? It almost feels good, doesn't it? . . . A hard hatred to gnaw on, to pour your bile over, crouched in your dark bunker, seething, remembering, pulling the unforgivable to your chest, embracing it, squeezing yourself into it, becoming it, becoming smaller . . . smaller . . .

Is a hatred consuming me, diminishing me, paralyzing me?
Is it squeezing me into a clot in a dark corner? Today I will
let it go. I will come up from the darkness and stretch out
in the sun, and I will walk tall again.

Archimedes was a mathematician who lived in Greece around 250 B.C. One day, while taking a bath, he finally figured out a problem that had been troubling him for ages.

—I Wonder Why Greeks Built Temples: and Other Questions About Ancient Greece
by Fiona Macdonald

That discovery became known as Archimedes' principle. It has to do with the relationship of weight to displaced fluid (in Archimedes' case, his body in the bathwater). Now, you may never come up with something as momentous as that, but there's a broader lesson here: Answers to your problems may be all around you, sometimes in the most ordinary places.

I'm pretty good at reading words, but can I "read" other things? Can I find answers to my questions in the ordinary trappings of my everyday life? I'll make a little game of it. I'll play Archimedes. I'll pick a question, then see if I can discover the answer . . . in the kitchen . . . or the backyard . . . or the bathtub. . . .

While there are many bad things about having a crush, just about the worst of them is the stupid things you will do because of it.

—"What's the Worst That Could Happen?"
by Bruce Coville
(from *13: Thirteen Stories That Capture the Agony and Ecstasy of Being Thirteen*, edited by James Howe)

So what's the point? Nobody should ever have a crush? No, not at all. Go ahead. Have your crush. Do your stupid things. Everyone is entitled to a little stupidity now and then. Just do yourself this favor: When it's all over, let the lessons you've learned inform you how to better handle the next crush.

The next crush I have on somebody will probably lead me to do something stupid. So be it. But I won't go totally bananas. I'll apply two controls on my crush behavior:
1. I won't be stupid in a way that hurts someone else.
2. I'll try to learn something from the experience.

My head spins so much when I think
of all that, I must stop.

—*Climbing the Stairs*
by Padma Venkatraman

It happens to everybody: You're drenched under a cloud-burst of life. School. Family. Friends. Clothes. Cavities. Long division. Your poor head is spinning. You're getting dizzy. What can you do?

I'll turn my back on all that, that's what I'll do. I'll walk away from the cloudburst. Go swimming. Play ball. Start a hobby. Do something physical, not brainy. Not forever. Just long enough to clear my head.

Soon, they couldn't agree on anything.

—*Together*
by Jane Simmons

And yet, notice the title: *Together.* Disagreement is not necessarily a reason to head for Splitsville. In fact, a relationship without disagreement is probably too brittle to last. Some of the best human bonds are forged in the fire of disagreement. Disagreement is to friendship as a barbell is to muscle: It may make you sore, but it will also make you strong.

In my relationships I won't go out of my way to disagree, but I won't shy away from it either. Disagreement is a sign of honest difference of opinion. If I can disagree with someone and still remain friends, I'll take it as a sign that the relationship is real, not fake.

Do you seriously believe
anything worthwhile can be had
merely for the wishing?

—*The Wizard in the Tree*
by Lloyd Alexander

Genies' lamps. Stars. Birthday candles. Before such things we close our eyes and make our wishes. We do it even though we know the real world doesn't work that way. We do it because it's fun. Because, for a moment or two, in spite of all we know, we get some sort of comfort from it. And we do it because playing this little game is actually one of life's clever ways of helping us identify what matters most to us. When we open our eyes, wishes end—and effort begins.

Sure, I wish for stuff. Who doesn't? But do I spend too much time on stars and birthday candles? Too much time waiting for a genie to come along? Am I letting my wishes fall abandoned into the black hole of the future—or am I backing them up with action?

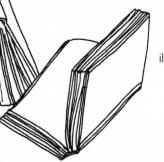

To anyone who'd listen
he liked to say, "The things
I want to know are in books."

—*Abe Lincoln:*
The Boy Who Loved Books
by Kay Winters
illustrated by Nancy Carpenter

Books are humanity's attic. They are where we save all the words, ideas, and stories that we can't bear to part with—that, collectively, define us. Everything worth knowing is somewhere in a book.

Today I will step back into history. I will experience something as old-fashioned as apple dunking, as time-honored as exploring the family attic, as priceless as an hour with Abe Lincoln. In other words, I will open a book and begin to read.

And from then on, both Kelly and Max worked hard to make their school a better place.

—*Max for President*
by Jarrett J. Krosoczka

You spend almost as much time at school as at home. Wouldn't you be happier there if it were a better place? Isn't there something you and your classmates can do about it? Why leave everything up to the faculty and staff and school board?

Hey, it's my school. Repeat: *my* school. So I'll talk to a few friends today and see if we can come up with an idea or two to improve the place.

In the ancient city of Rome there lived a humble and gentle man. . . . The man's friends and neighbors called him Valentine.

—*Saint Valentine*
retold and illustrated by Robert Sabuda

In another story of ancient Rome, Shakespeare's play *Julius Caesar*, Roman general Mark Antony says, "The evil that men do lives after them; the good is oft interred with their bones." Saint Valentine is a happy exception. At a time when the Roman emperor forbade his troops to marry, Valentine the priest continued to perform weddings for soldiers and the women they loved. Almost two thousand years after he died, we exchange candy, cards, and other expressions of love and affection in his name.

Saint Valentine didn't invent love and affection. But he did give us an occasion to express them. There are people in this world whom I love. This is the day above all others to show it. I will.

There's no official limit on
how many friends a [kid] can have.

—*A Smart Girl's Guide to Friendship Troubles*
(American Girl Library)
by Patti Kelley Criswell
illustrated by Angela Martini

First off, we're talking boys as well as girls here. Whichever you are, don't confine yourself to a select group of friends, often known as a clique. Cliques by definition leave people out. Lock yourself into one, and you'll never know how many terrific friendships you may be missing.

I love my buddies, and I love to spend time with them. But I will not allow them to dictate who is and is not an acceptable friend for me. Today I'll take a look at a bunch of kids I barely know and see if I can identify one as a potential new friend.

The whole afternoon Ruby kept quiet.
Her mother wondered if she were sick.
But Ruby wasn't sick. She had the blues.

—*Ruby Sings the Blues*
by Niki Daly

You could have told Ruby's mother that, couldn't you? "That girl's not sick. She's got the blues." And it's no small thing, you might add. Because the blues come in one size only. Ruby's blues—and *your* blues—are every bit as *big* and as *bad* and as *blue* as a grown-up's. And how do grown-ups handle their blues? By sharing them. With a good friend—who may or may not be their mother.

**If I'm blue today, I'll share my feelings
with someone I trust.**

Kindness comes with no price.

—*Tongues of Jade*
by Laurence Yep
illustrated by David Wiesner

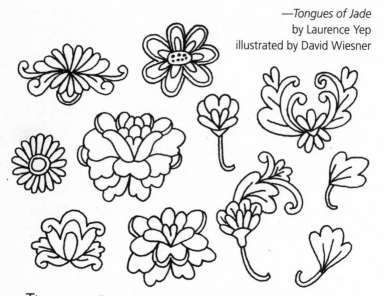

They say talk is cheap. Maybe so. But kindness is even better—it's free! Free to give. Free to receive. Makes you wonder why there's not more of it, huh?

I'll make sure February 17th lives up to its name.
And it won't cost me a penny!

I t gave him an extra heartbeat to . . .
understand that grace is given.

—*What Hearts*
by Bruce Brooks

Grace is a hard word to pin down. On this page, let's consider it another word for "blessing." Someone you think doesn't like you smiles at you. A kid you just beat at something says "Nice game." It's your turn to give your talk to the class and you're a basket case of nerves and the kid across the aisle catches your eye and nods. Grace. There's only one way to get it: It must be given to you. You may think you don't deserve it, but if you get it, cherish it. Grace. Tiny blessings. A gift.

Will grace come my way today? Will I even know it
if it happens? If so, I will be grateful, as I would be
for any gift. And looking at this from the other direction—
is there someone whose life might become a little better
with a tiny blessing from me?

"Not everything you hear about people is true."

—*Lizzie Logan Wears Purple Sunglasses*
by Eileen Spinelli
illustrated by Melanie Hope Greenberg

We all agree, right? Nobody disputes the above statement—in theory, at least. But how many of us, in practice, live by it? When we hear something nasty about someone, how often do we assume it's true?

Today, as on almost every other day, I'll probably hear something bad about somebody. Maybe just a little thing, maybe a really huge rotten thing. I may be tempted to believe it just on the speaker's say-so, but I'll resist the temptation. I'll take a page from our system of justice: innocent until *proven* guilty.

"Yes! Visiting is nice," Muktuk says.
"Who shall we visit?" Irving says.

—*Bad Bears Go Visiting*
by Daniel Pinkwater
illustrated by Jill Pinkwater

OK, so visiting doesn't seem like a big deal to you. You're constantly surrounded by people. You spend most of your waking hours in the presence of family and friends. (Do enemies count?) But maybe that's not the case with everyone. Maybe some people spend their days pretty much alone. Maybe one little visit from somebody would make their day.

Do I know someone who could use a visit? Someone
who lives alone? It's in my power to make someone
like that very happy simply by paying him or her a visit.
Today I'll use that power.

Welcome to Writing Your Life.

—Writing Your Life:
An Easy-to-Follow Guide
to Writing an Autobiography
by Mary Borg

il was born on April

No person on earth is so boring and insignificant that he or she is not worth writing or reading about. Maybe you're not putting it down on paper, but each passing day is a page that you add to the story of your life. So what are you? A thriller? A mystery? A comedy? A romance? A drama? One thing's for sure—no one but you can be the hero of your story.

Today I will make a list of ten interesting things about myself. If I don't feel like stopping there, maybe I'll go on and write a book: The Story of Me.

George Washington was discouraged.

—*When Washington Crossed the Delaware*
by Lynne Cheney
illustrated by Peter M. Fiore

Huh? The "Father of Our Country"? The guy on Mount Rushmore? The guy who threw a silver dollar across the Potomac? *That* George Washington? *Discouraged?* Yeah, discouraged. Believe it. And here's the moral of this tale: Great achievement goes through, not around, discouragement.

Is there a roadblock in my way, keeping me
from something I want to achieve? Am I discouraged?
I understand now that discouragement often precedes
achievement. Instead of retreating from the roadblock
or seeking a way around it, I will boldly punch a hole
through it and continue toward my goal.

I believe I love my family
but sometimes I can't stand them,
and they can't stand me. . . .

—*What I Believe*
by Norma Fox Mazer

The character who wrote the lines above may be wiser than she realizes. Because she already seems to understand that family life can be an apparent contradiction: Love and "can't stand" inhabit the same house. The fact that she not only recognizes this but admits it suggests that her family is pretty open and honest about their relationships. They express to one another both their loving feelings and their not-so-loving feelings. This is good. This is healthy.

Am I mad at my family today? If so, it's OK, it's only natural. I shouldn't be afraid to admit it to myself—or to them. Openness and honesty are as important to my family's health as brushing is to my teeth. Love is big. Love makes room for conflicting feelings.

Grandpa loves
bare feet and bagels.
Coffee with cream.
Flipping the pancakes
and mornings
with me.

—*Grandpa Loves*
by Rebecca Kai Dotlich
illustrated by Kathryn Brown

With me. These words keep recurring in the book. Because no matter what a grandparent does, it's almost always best when done with a grandchild.

My grandparents like to do things with me, go places
with me. How long has it been since I told them
I like it, too? If it's been longer than yesterday—or
never—I'll say it real soon.

She had eyes in the back of her heart.

—*A Year Down Yonder*
by Richard Peck

Isn't that a nice phrase? It reminds us that vision is not limited to the eyes in the head, nor even the front of the heart. It reminds us that no one's hurt is too small, no worry too removed, no blessing so elusive that it cannot be seen by the eyes in the back of the human heart.

As I am being watched by unseen eyes, I am reminded that I, too, have unseen eyes, eyes that can see the pain behind a smile, the fear in bravado, the affection in a criticism.
Today I will open *all* of my eyes.

Pictures are music for the eyes.

—*Looking at Paintings: An Introduction
to Fine Art for Young People*
by Erika Langmuir

Nobody had to teach you to like music. Your favorite musical styles, your favorite songs, simply and naturally became part of your life. You can hook up with art just as naturally. Give it a chance. Check it out. Something will ring your chimes.

The world is full of great art. How much longer am I going to ignore it? Today I'll ask my parents to take me to an art museum. My eyes deserve it.

Saying "no" is not uncommon for Violet.

—*Violet Bing and the Grand House*
by Jennifer Paros

Keep this in mind: Every time you say *no* to something, you're also saying *yes* to something else. Saying *no* to cheating, for example, is saying *yes* to integrity and self-respect. Saying *no* to drugs is saying *yes* to an independent, healthy future.

It's time I take inventory of my decisions. Is *no* common or uncommon for me? What *yeses* am I passing up because I don't say *no* enough?

"I've never told anyone,"
Great-grandma said, "but I've always
wanted a pair of red shoes."

—*The Secret of the Red Shoes: A Story About
an Elderly Great-Grandmother*
by Joan Donaldson
illustrated by Doris Ettlinger

Three points here:

1. *Listen* to other people. It's how you find out what they like—so you can surprise them and not have to ask "What do you want for your birthday?"

2. Give people what *they* want to receive, not what *you* want to give.

3. Don't think that because your grandmother or great-grandmother is "old" she no longer likes to wear cool stuff.

I'll get gift-giving ideas from listening, and I'll give people what they want—even if it's red shoes for Great-grandma.

Each Leap Day, my leapmates and I
send each other gifts.

—*Leap Day*
by Wendy Mass

If you were a Leap Day baby—"Happy birthday to you. . . ."
How does it feel to have a date all to yourself (almost)? You
belong to a pretty exclusive group. Why don't you check
around, see if you can discover a few of your datemates?

And if I do find one or more—young or old, male or
female, near or far—I'll ask if they'd like to exchange gifts
or otherwise celebrate our special once-every-four-years day.

"I have heard so many convincing doomsday predictions that I should have seen the world end at least six times in my lifetime."

—*Starbright and the Dream Eater*
by Joy Cowley

Naysayers and doomsdayers—what would we do without them? By telling us we are bound to fail, they inspire us to succeed. By telling us the world is a rotten place that's going to end tomorrow, they turn our attention to what's good and beautiful today. Call it social ecology: Like wasps, even "No" people have their place.

Tell me about it. I've already got "No" people in my life. Always complaining. Finding fault. Never satisfied. Always putting other people down, including me. One of these days I'm going to thank them for providing a public service.

*O*nce upon a time, there lived a boy
who feasted on books and was wild
about animals. . . . All in all,
he excelled at fooling around.

—*The Boy on Fairfield Street*
by Kathleen Krull
paintings by Steve Johnson and Lou Fancher

You're looking at the name up there by the date, and
you're thinking "Who's Ted Geisel?" Right? Well, maybe
you know him better as . . . Dr. Seuss.

Little Teddy Geisel wasn't born with a tag on his toe
saying "World-Famous Author." He was just another kid
on Fairfield Street. A fool-around kid. In many ways
just like me. My assignment today doesn't require me
to get up out of this chair or even out of bed.
All I have to do is wonder—wonder what sort of
interesting person I might become.

"I was constantly surrounded by chances to do wrong," [Jackie] said. "Success seemed a distant dream."

—*50 American Heroes Every Kid Should Meet*
by Dennis Denenberg and Lorraine Roscoe

No one dragged Jackie Joyner-Kersee to the Olympic medal stand. All along the way, especially in her younger years, she turned her back on temptation, saying "No" to the wrong way. Success is as much about *don't* as about *do*.

I want to succeed. But life won't necessarily make it easy for me. Chances to do wrong will tempt me. If one tempts me today, I will say "No."

"I just felt like . . . like everyone was looking at me, expecting great things, and that no matter how well I played, it wouldn't be good enough."

—*Boys in Control*
by Phyllis Reynolds Naylor

Pressure like this comes from one of two sources: (a) yourself or (b) others. Or maybe even both. In any case, the solution lies in the sanctuary of concentration. Bypass your expectations and those of others and zero in on the task itself, whether it be a chorus solo, a foul shot, or a part in the school play. Submerge yourself totally in what you are doing. Don't let expectations sabotage your best effort.

Of course I don't want to disappoint people—or myself—with a poor showing. And that's why I will practice concentration as well as performance. So that when the time comes, it will be just me and my task out there, doing our best, letting expectations take care of themselves.

My master fails to notice,
Though I know that he is smart,
The incalculable sadness
Deep within my dragon heart.

—"I Am My Master's Dragon"
The Dragons Are Singing Tonight
by Jack Prelutsky
illustrated by Peter Sís

Yes, a dragon can be sad. And a big, tough kid might be afraid of birds. And a prom queen can feel unattractive. And a quiet kid might sing in the shower. And the kid who laughs all day might cry all night.

Today I will be wary of appearances. I will make no assumptions about others—except that there is more to them than meets my eye.

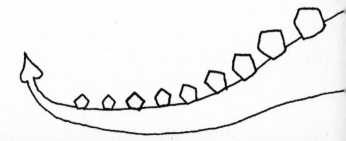

Never laugh at anyone's religion,
because whether you take it seriously
or not, they do.

—*The Long Secret*
by Louise Fitzhugh

Laughter is the first resort of the ignorant. Maybe you don't agree with someone else's religion. Maybe you think it's weird or goofy. Maybe you just don't get it. You don't have to. All you have to do is respect the other person's right to believe in something that you don't.

Whether or not I believe in God—whether I go
by the name of Christian or Jew or Muslim or whatever—
I will grant everyone else the respect that I
expect them to show me.

"Mom, I found this dog sitting all by himself. Can I keep him?"

—*Can I Keep Him?*
by Steven Kellogg

Every day the world over, kids come home with a stray animal and plead, "Can I keep him? Pleeeeze!" But how many kids go on to say, "I'll be totally responsible for him. I'll take care of him. I'll feed him. I promise."

OK, so maybe I want a pet. But how about what the pet wants and needs? Am I ready and willing to take responsibility? Or will I dump it onto my parents when the novelty wears off? I'll hold off pleading my case until I have the right answers to these questions.

If we cannot serve in one way,
there is always another.

—*The Door in the Wall*
by Marguerite de Angeli

Do your efforts go unnoticed? Do you show up to do a good deed and find it's already been done by somebody else? Does no one seem to want what you have to offer? All the world asks of you is that you be willing to serve. Service truly offered is like water: It flows toward every need. Be patient. Be ready. Be willing. The call will come.

There are opportunities all around me, good things needing to be done. Maybe I just haven't been seeing them. Today I'll look in different places.

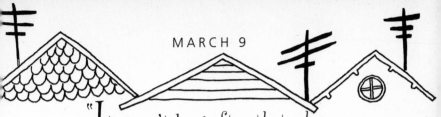

"It wasn't long after that when television antennas started to sprout from the rooftops like weeds in the springtime. And the more they grew, the fewer boys and girls came out to listen to my stories."

—*Kamishibai Man*
by Allen Say

TV is a relentless tyrant. It bullies other diversions and seeks to swallow every minute you can spare and some you can't. It holds you captive in its glowing eye until you forget the wonders of live theater, the cozy solitude of reading a book, the whisper and lilt of a storyteller.

When I'm not plopped in front of a computer or video game, am I plopped in front of a TV? Have I been duped into thinking TV is the only way to admit stories into my life? What other forms of storytelling am I missing just because I refuse to click the Off button on the TV remote?
. . . Click.

And so Colin had come down,
delighted to be needed.

—*The Various*
by Steve Augarde

When someone asks for a favor, do you get grumpy and resentful and reluctant? Or does it make you feel good to know that you're needed?

Requests for favors don't always come at the most convenient times. I might be busy with something else. Or dozing off. I might forget to feel flattered that someone is depending on me. I might not be tuned in to how good it feels to be needed. If someone asks me for a favor today, I'll try to give the right answer.

Spoon was afraid of losing what little was left of her—his memories. He was afraid of forgetting her.

—*Sun & Spoon*
by Kevin Henkes

And that's why, if you read on, Spoon searches for a keepsake to remind him forever of his beloved grandmother. Memories, feelings, the indescribable spark of life itself—all comprise the human experience, yet you can hold none in your hand. We crave mementos we can see and touch. The most common, never-noticed possessions of someone who is gone forever—or on a long vacation or business trip—become treasured remembrances.

Could I ever forget any member of my family? Of course not. But why don't I show my affection for them in a touchable way, right now? Why don't I collect from each of them a little, living keepsake and put them in a special place in my room? Someday I'll be glad I did.

When people come up with new ideas,
they have to have confidence in
themselves to say, "I CAN DO IT!"

—*The Hero Book: Learning Lessons from the People You Admire*
by Ellen Sabin

New ideas are wonderful things, rare and special. When someone has one, there should be a parade. And a headline in the paper: JANE SMITH GETS NEW IDEA! Sadly, many new ideas are dumped in the trash. Why? Because new ideas scare us. And because we figure: If I'm the only one to come up with this new idea, it can't be very special. Who do I think I am? Einstein?

If I get a new idea today—or any day—I won't run
from it. I won't trash it. If it's something I really
want to do—I'll do it. (Who knows, maybe
it will lead to a parade someday.)

...and then she told him...

I have long since learned
not to believe idle stories.

—*An Unlikely Friendship:
A Novel of Mary Todd Lincoln and Elizabeth Keckley*
by Ann Rinaldi

You hear a lot in the hallways, in the lunchroom, after school, on weekends. How much of it do you believe? All of it? Half? Ten percent? Many untruths are told by people who are not liars. They simply don't know they're not telling the truth—because they believe an untruth passed on to them by somebody else. An untruth is like a germ: It can infect everyone who comes in contact with it.

Bad things about other people—I hear this stuff all the time. How much of it is true? How much do I believe? Starting today, I won't believe these things until they pass several tests:

- How trustworthy is the person saying it?
- Can it be verified by others or by me?
- What do my own best instincts and common sense have to say about it?
- Is my judgment impaired because I'm too anxious to believe it?

"Spring's come early! Let's celebrate!"

—*Groundhog Stays Up Late*
by Margery Cuyler
illustrated by Jean Cassels

It's been a long, cold winter, and one of these mornings you'll discover you don't have to button up when you leave the house. You'll spy purple and yellow crocuses peeping up from a neighbor's yard. And a thin veil of green on some of the trees. Hey, you know spring when you see it, but the calendar says *Not yet*. Does that mean you've got to wait till March 21st to feel good about all this? to shout "Yahoo! It's spring!"?

In two words: *Heck no.* Because life doesn't always happen according to a timetable or calendar. And feelings can't be scheduled. So as soon as I see that first crocus . . .
"YAHOO!"

When I'm sad, my mother gives me fruit and a glass of milk. Then we talk.

—*Sly the Sleuth and the Food Mysteries*
by Donna Jo Napoli and Robert Furrow
illustrated by Heather Maione

There are weddings and funerals and graduations and initiations and all sorts of other rituals, many of them centuries old and lavish and very public. But some of the most useful rituals are those we design ourselves. A good way to deal with a bad day is to frame it in a ritual of your own making. If you're feeling sad, for example, you might listen to a favorite piece of music or read a poem you love or go to a special place. Doing so may help to contain a problem that feels as if it is spilling all over you.

I'll keep this in mind next time I feel a sadness or some other problem spilling over me. My ritual may be fruit, milk, and a talk with Mom—or it may be totally different. I will seek a familiar, comforting shape into which to pour my problem.

Sometimes a person needs a quiet place.

—*A Quiet Place*
by Douglas Wood
illustrated by Dan Andreasen

Do you hear it? The voice? It's your own self. No, not the big, blustery, public one. The soft one. The little one. The whisper one. It's trying to reach you.

Yesterday, and the day before, I think my whisper voice tried to reach me. But I did not hear. Today I will get myself to a quiet place, and I will listen. Today I will hear.

For the McKeevers were
down on their luck.

—*The Leprechaun in the Basement*
by Kathy Tucker
illustrated by John Sanford

Is your family down on its luck, going through hard times? financial problems? physical problems? emotional problems? Just as good times are more fun when they are shared, so hard times are a little easier to bear when they are shared by all. Going through hard times doesn't mean you have to go around monkey-faced all day, but it does mean you should pitch in to help turn your family back up on its luck.

Next time hard times hit my family, I won't just go off on my own happy little tangent. I'll ask Mom and Dad how I can help.

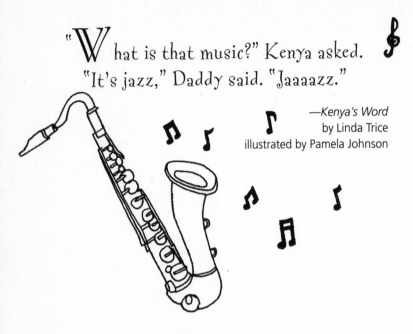

"What is that music?" Kenya asked.
"It's jazz," Daddy said. "Jaaaazz."

—*Kenya's Word*
by Linda Trice
illustrated by Pamela Johnson

Maybe you'll like it, maybe you won't. But give it a try. Take a taste. It comes in many flavors, including Dixieland, ragtime, swing, bebop, and cool. It's America's music. It was invented here. It's jazz.

I hereby declare this week Jazz Week. Each day for seven days I'll take at least ten minutes to listen to a different "flavor" of jazz. There may be some new music in my future.

Even the queen is obliged to take a holiday from her cares and woes.

—*The Queen's Progress:*
An Elizabethan Alphabet
by Celeste Davidson Mannis
illustrated by Bagram Ibatoulline

If it's good enough for the queen, it's good enough for you. Give yourself a break. Go on vacation. Be sure *not* to pack your cares and woes. Don't worry—they'll still be there when you return. Or, if you prefer, stay home and send your cares and woes on an all-expenses-paid trip around the world. As every queen knows, either way works.

Today I'll give my biggest care the day off.

"I . . . errr," I say. "I mean . . .
ummm . . . yeah."

—*The Earth, My Butt and Other Big Round Things*
by Carolyn Mackler

If most of us could see our everyday conversations in writing, we'd be shocked. They would be hardly readable. And suddenly we would begin to understand why communication is such a big problem.

If it's possible, just for fun, I'll record some conversation between me and my friends. Then I'll transcribe five or ten minutes' worth. I'm curious to see how much sense it will make and what I might learn about communicating better.

I would not climb any stairs if I were
Masai. I would lift a cowhide flap, and
I'd be home.

—*Masai and I*
by Virginia Kroll
illustrated by Nancy Carpenter

The narrator in this story, Linda, imagines herself as a Masai girl in East Africa. What a wonderful detail, a telling difference, to enter a house by lifting a cowhide flap instead of turning a doorknob. If we can't travel the world and do such things in person, the next-best thing is to imagine and read about them. And why bother? Because in a world too much at odds with itself, harmony follows knowledge.

Today I'll choose some country, some culture, I've never before given a moment's thought to. I'll read about these other people, how they're both different from me and the same as me. It is good to know my earthly neighbors.

"How about a drink?" "What can I get you?" "Want a beer?"

—*Drinking: A Risky Business*
by Laurence Pringle

If you haven't been asked these questions yet, sooner or later you will be. Will you have the right answers ready? Understand, this book doesn't presume to tell you how to run the rest of your life. The idea is to help you successfully navigate your kid-time. If you want a beer when you're twenty-five, this book says it's your call. But for now . . .

. . . For now, my answers to the questions above are
as follows:

1. No.
2. Fruit juice.
3. No.

"It doesn't matter
if you're an amateur
or a pro poet. Nobody knows
until they try it. . . ."

—*Sister Slam and the Poetic Motormouth Road Trip*
by Linda Oatman High

Are you a poet but you don't know it? A painter without a brush? A dancer with no stage? Hey, this is it—*right now!*—the time when you find out who you are and what you can do. And how will you ever know if you don't try new stuff? Forget the time on clock and calendar. It's Try New Stuff time!

How will I know what I can do and can't do, what I do and don't like, if I never try anything new? Today I'll try a new thing. And next week another new thing. And every week for a year. Because the time is always TNS time!

If Houdini could hold his breath for five thousand seconds in his crate in the ocean, then Victor could certainly hold his breath for five thousand seconds in his tub in the bathroom.

—*The Houdini Box*
by Brian Selznick

It doesn't take Victor long to discover that he cannot match his role model, Houdini. Role models are good only if they are used correctly. You cannot expect to master instantly what they have taken years to achieve through hard work and practice. Neither they nor anyone else can transfer their achievement to you. What a role model *can* do is inspire you to spend the time and effort to achieve a goal of your own.

I will not try to become my role model. I will use my role model to try to become a better me.

When David gets in trouble, he always says . . . "No! It's not my fault!"

—*David Gets in Trouble*
by David Shannon

Flip Wilson, a famous comedian, used to crack "The Devil made me do it!" and the audience laughed because they recognized their own tendency to blame their screwups on anybody but themselves. Think about it: When was the last time you saw someone stand up and say, "I did it. It's my fault"? Now think about this: If you ever do witness such a miracle, don't you think you'll really respect that person?

Why don't I ever put the blame on myself?
What am I afraid of—respect? If I screw up today,
I'll point the finger at myself.

"But I know you are telling me
the truth, Ben."

—*The Angel's Command*
by Brian Jacques
illustrated by David Elliot

Do people trust you enough to say that if you say so, it must be true?

I hope so. I'll try to make it so.

Yet I'm sometimes impatient, sad, angry. . . .

—*Brown Honey in Broomwheat Tea*
by Joyce Carol Thomas
illustrated by Floyd Cooper

In other words, she's human. Anyone who doesn't have negative emotions isn't real. The point here isn't what to do about negative emotions—see other pages for that; the point is simply that it's natural to sometimes have them. OK?

Syllogism: Bad feelings are part of being human; I'm human; therefore, bad feelings are part of me. I won't coop them up. I won't apologize for having them. I'll give them some slack, let them express themselves.
It's part of who I am. It's OK.

Bear in mind that it is not fine clothes that make the gentleman.

—*The Adventures of Pinocchio*
by Carlo Collodi

Or, we might add, the lady. Clothes are a stupendously un-reliable way to measure a person's quality. Labels, price tags, brand names—ignore them all. The true worth of your classmates will show through their words and deeds, not their clothes.

Today when I meet someone wearing expensive clothes, I will resist being impressed. When I meet someone wearing cheap clothes, I will resist feeling superior.

You can't take [words] back. . . .
They sit there like big damp frogs.

—*Western Wind*
by Paula Fox

And those frogs croak all night long. You can't shut them up. You can hold your mouth open for the next ten years and they will not hop back in. Happily, there is one foolproof protection against regretted word-frogs: Don't let them out in the first place.

Today, if I feel myself about to release a word I'll regret, I'll bite my frog.

S ome days sting
and others pour like sugar
from your spoon.

—"Squeeze"
Squeeze: Poems from a Juicy Universe
by Heidi Mordhorst
illustrated by Jesse Torrey

Some days are so bad you're afraid they'll never end, others so good you *wish* they'd never end. That's days for you—not much you can do about them. But there is something you do have control over: your attitude. When your day is pouring like sugar, you can cherish and live every moment of it to the fullest. And when your day stings, you can take comfort in knowing there may be sugar on the other side of midnight.

Will my today be sting or sugar? Whichever, I've got
an attitude ready to handle it.

A ngel decided to make the most beautiful kite in the world.

—Angel's Kite: La estrella de Ángel
by Alberto Blanco
illustrated by Rodolfo Morales

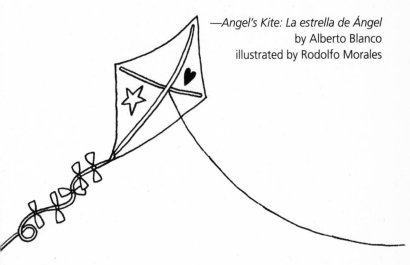

Angel, what's the matter with you? Don't you know we don't—gulp!—*make* things? We *buy* things. Did you ever hear of *stores*? the *mall*? It's where you *buy* everything you *need*. Hello? Anybody home in there? What kind of kid are you, anyway?

Today I will find out what kind of kid Angel is. I will make a list of three things that I can *make* instead of *buy*.

W hen it came time for Miss Higgins
to give out grades, she kept
remembering the student who had
brought her a pastrami sandwich.

—*Forget Apples; or My Report Card, My Menu*
by A. P. Phull

"There appears to be a direct correlation between the grade awarded the student and the gift given the teacher—especially when the gift is food." These are the concluding words of a recent study investigating students' ability to influence their teachers in the matter of grades. The most successful students (A- to A+) were found to offer gifts only after thoroughly researching their teacher's eating preferences.

It's tough on teachers, having to make all those decisions on grades with nothing to go on but homework, test scores, and classroom participation. They need help. I'll help my teacher decide my grade with a gift. Pickles to pork rolls— whatever it takes—I'll meet the challenge.*

* April Fool's! You can't grub grades with food. (It doesn't hurt to be nice to your teacher, though.)

I saw a little girl in a wooden wagon . . .
staring at the rising sun as if it were
the very dawn of creation.

—*Love, Stargirl*
by Jerry Spinelli

Why let the sun do all the dawning?

I'll give this day a second sunrise: I'll smile.

Put me in a blindfold
so I can't see a thing.
Even with my eyes closed
I'll still know it's spring.

—"Nose Knows"
Pieces: A Year in Poems & Quilts
by Anna Grossnickle Hines

We all come in a package. It's called the body. It's surprising how little we know about it, how little we appreciate its ability to inform us of the world around us—including spring and a million other things.

Today I'm going to get to know my senses better.
I'm going to close my eyes for ten minutes. Then I'll
pinch my nose and muffle my ears for ten minutes each.
This will help me do two things:
1. appreciate the rewards of my missing sense;
2. appreciate the surprising, compensating powers
of my other senses.

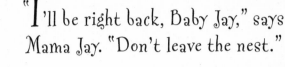

"I'll be right back, Baby Jay," says Mama Jay. "Don't leave the nest."

—*Leaving the Nest*
by Mordicai Gerstein

"Stay put."
"Don't leave the house."
"Don't open the door."
"Don't talk to strangers."
"Call me when you get there."

Parental directions are not intended to hassle you. They're intended to keep you safe. Heed them—until it's time for you to leave the nest.

Heeding my parents' directions has kept me safe so far.
I'll keep on heeding, and I'll remember this when
I have a nest—and nestlings—of my own.

... I didn't know what to say
so I wiggled my nose and made my bunny face
and she laughed. . . .

—"Making Friends"
In the Land of Words: New and Selected Poems
by Eloise Greenfield
illustrated by Jan Spivey Gilchrist

The poem goes on to say they both made faces and they both laughed and then . . . "we were friends." One of the best things about life is friends. We all agree on that. And yet our shyness with strangers often prevents friendship from ever gaining a foothold. If only we would realize that the other person is probably just as shy as we are and is simply waiting—and hoping—for us to make the first move.

I'm not very good at bunny faces—and I'm too old for that,
anyway—but I can do a killer [you supply the move].
Today I'll pick out a stranger and give it a try.
A new friend may be only a killer move away.

Give yourself to the rain when it falls.

—*Give Yourself to the Rain: Poems for the Very Young*
by Margaret Wise Brown
illustrated by Teri L. Weidner

Little kids have the right idea—they splash in puddles and dance in rain. What is it about growing up that makes us treat the rain like falling porcupine needles? Ban umbrellas! Go dance with the little kids. It's your birthright. Your earth-right.

If it rains today, I'll run outside.

As Mrs. Del Rubio stamped the book, she said, "Remember to return it by April seventh."

—*Beverly Billingsly Borrows a Book*
by Alexander Stadler

OK, so returning a library book on time is not exactly the Biggest Deal in This Book. But look at it this way: When you return something you've borrowed, you are completing a circle of trust. And trust, more than money, is the soundest currency of all.

Have I borrowed a book—or anything else—lately?
If so, I'll make sure not only to return it
but to return it on time.

Later in life Alec said he learned to be
observant during his long walks
to and from school.

—*With a Little Luck: Surprising Stories of Amazing Discoveries*
by Dennis Brindell Fradin

Walk? Did someone say *walk*? Aren't we the species that
rides everywhere, whose babies ten million years from now
will probably be born with wheels instead of feet? Take a
deep breath and repeat this three times:

I have feet. I can walk.

I have feet. I can walk.

I have feet. I can walk.

Try it, and guess what: You'll see stuff you never knew
was there.

Today I'm going to—gulp!—walk. Maybe to or from
school—or through a park—or just around the block.
I look forward to seeing the little things
I've been missing all my life.

For those who are willing to make
an effort, great miracles and
wonderful treasures are in store.

—"A Tale of Three Wishes"
Stories for Children
by Isaac Bashevis Singer

Branch Rickey, a great baseball man, said it another way: "Luck is the residue of design." Good things, even miracles, have a way of happening only when we're up off our duff and doing something. Fortune seldom falls to couch potatoes.

Do I spend too much time on my duff, doing nothing? Do I consider watching TV and hanging out "doing something"? OK, so I don't have to run a marathon today, but as long as I'm making an effort at something productive, I'm putting myself in a position to get the most out of my life.

"Be patient, Mayumie.
We're almost there."

—*The Falling Flowers*
by Jennifer B. Reed
illustrated by Dick Cole

Kids—little kids especially—have a problem with patience. When they go on trips, they're famous for saying every five minutes "Are we there yet?" Mayumie is no exception as she rides the train to Tokyo with her grandmother. When they arrive, as usually happens, Mayumie discovers that the wait was well worth it.

Many good things await your arrival as you ride toward adulthood. Immerse yourself in the days along the way and you will arrive in plenty of time. Be patient.

Have I said "Are we there yet?" for the last time? Am I ready to stop itching and fretting because every little thing isn't happening *right this instant*? Am I old enough to be patient?

"You understand now that the more you give, the more you have left to give?"

—*Sharing Susan*
by Eve Bunting

What kind of goofy talk is this? Subtraction becomes addition? If you have a quarter in your pocket and you give it to someone in need, are you supposed to believe that another quarter magically appears in your pocket? Well, maybe not, but only because it was more than the quarter that you gave. The quarter, you see, was just a symbol, a token of a much bigger gift—the gift of your heart, your humanity. And, yes, the more you give of your heart, the more of it there is to give.

Inside me is a miracle waiting to happen, call it my heart, my spirit, my humanity, whatever. If I try to save it and hoard it all for myself, it only shrinks smaller and smaller. But if I give it away—lo and behold, it grows! I could give for a thousand years and never use up half of my heart.

Symmetry is a state of balance.

—*Math for Kids & Other People Too!*
by Theoni Pappas

One kid loves to read but is totally lost on a ball field. Another kid is on the cell phone all day—instead of doing homework or walking the dog or eating. Kids like this are out of balance. One-sided. It's a shame. If you're one of them, you're forgetting that one of the best things about being a kid is that you don't have to go off to a specialized job every day. You'll have plenty of time for that when you grow up. For now, use your kid-time. You can do lots of different things, all in the same day, the same week. This is symmetry. This is balance. It's your kidright. Use it.

Is my life out of balance? Am I tilting too much one way or another? Let it be known that yesterday was the last day I was one-sided.

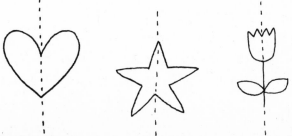

Since Miss Hagerty appreciates beauty, I put a pansy in a bud vase in the corner of her tray.

—*A Corner of the Universe*
by Ann M. Martin

Many life lessons can be found in this simple gesture. Let's focus on just two: sensitivity and action. That is, (1) being aware of what others like and (2) acting on it.

Am I a kind, sensitive, giving person? Sometimes it's hard to know, because for much of my life these qualities have been assignments handed down from my parents: "Write a thank-you note to Aunt Sally." . . . "Tell Grandma she looks nice in her new outfit." . . . and so on. Today, if only to prove to myself that I can do it, I'll aim my sensitivity at someone and see what I come up with.

Then I'll do something nice— *without* being told.

"Nobody believed the *Titanic* could sink. . . .
That's why none of the passengers believed
the ship was sinking, right up until
the last minute, until it was too late."

—*White Star: A Dog on the* Titanic
by Marty Crisp

People believed that the *Titanic* was unsinkable because that's what the shipbuilder told them. It's called marketing. Sometimes marketing claims are true; sometimes they're not. Marketing is often disguised as information, but its real purpose is to persuade you to buy something. Keep this in mind, whether you're shopping for mouthwash or an ocean cruise.

Today, like every day, I'll be bombarded by marketers promising me everything from clear skin to popularity. I'll begin by not believing everything they say. Then I'll test their claims against my own common sense and the experience of others. And finally I'll ask myself: Do I really need—or even want—this product?

"Do not boast," Bellini said.

—*Mirette on the High Wire*
by Emily Arnold McCully

Boasters make a big mistake: They think their boasting impresses others. But it doesn't. What impresses others is action. If the actions are not impressive, boasting only makes them less so.

I will not make the boasters' mistake. I'll shut my mouth and let my actions do the talking.

Nobody can be uncheered with a balloon.

—*Eeyore Has a Birthday*
by A. A. Milne
illustrated by Ernest H. Shepard

Sad to say, that's not always true, is it? Many a balloon has floated over a grumpy, cheerless face. But note this: Usually the grump is a grown-up. Little kids rarely fail to respond to a balloon—and in so doing, they send a message to us bigger people: Don't let yourself get so big and old and hard that a balloon, or any of life's other cheer-bringers, can't make you smile.

The things that used to cheer me up, do they still make me smile? If not, today I'll blow up a balloon and get reacquainted with the little kid in me.

Nothing in the world is quite
as adorably lovely as a robin
when he shows off. . . .

—*The Secret Garden*
by Frances Hodgson Burnett

Are you "adorably lovely" when you show off? Or only when you're sleeping (as your parents might say)? But think about it. What's a robin really doing when it shows off? Is it deliberately putting on a show? Not at all. It's simply being its own best self. That's all that's needed to be adorably lovely—sleeping or not.

Today I will be my own best self.

"Look around," said Gabby.
"It's a dump!"

—*The Messy Lot*
by Larry Dane Brimner
illustrated by Christine Tripp

And it *is* a dump: discarded tire, bike wheel, paint can, garbage, broken furniture. Right there in Gabby's neighborhood. So what does Gabby do? Wait for the Fairy Dumpmother to come along and clean up the mess? Or does she pitch in and do something about it?

I live in a house, but I also live on a street, in a neighborhood. Maybe it doesn't look like a dump, but sometimes I'll see a soda can or a Cracker Jack box or an apple core on the sidewalk, and, of course, I just walk by— like everybody else. Maybe for just one day in the year I might not be everybody else. Maybe one day in the year I might walk the length of my one little block with a bag and pick up trash. Maybe today.

"Feelings stink," he declared.
"This school stinks."

—*The Twinkie Squad*
by Gordon Korman

Now, what's a nasty quote like that doing in a nice book like this? Here's a kid who thinks life stinks. What's to be learned from that? Just this: At one time or another, we all think life stinks. It's natural. It's practically impossible to omit such moods totally from our lives. But maybe we can at least manage them. For instance: Make a deal that you'll allow yourself such a mood at the end of a really bad day but that you will never drag it into the next morning.

Will this turn out to be one of those really bad days that make me want to say "Life stinks"? If it is, so be it. But right now I pledge that when I wake up tomorrow morning, life and I will have a fresh start.

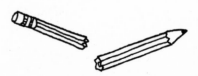

My advice to young poets is
"Look to your own lives."

—*A Fire in My Hands*
by Gary Soto

You are fascinating. No kidding. You've been living inside your own skin for so long, maybe you don't see it. Try this. Sit in a chair. Settle in. Get good and comfy. Now release your eyes. Let them go. Let them float out of your head and over there to the other side of the room. Now, when they look back, what do they see? They see a person who's different from every other creature that's ever been born. Someone with a unique history. Someone with friends and family and memories and dreams and triumphs and failures and fears and embarrassments and secrets. So, yeah: You're fascinating.

Today I am going to write a poem about myself, and there's only one place I need to turn to for research: little ol' fascinating me.

$H$is reply was discouraging.

—*Charlotte Brontë and Jane Eyre*
by Stewart Ross
illustrated by Robert Van Nutt

You hear lots of grown-ups say "Don't be discouraged." Yeah, right. While you're at it, why don't you tell me "Don't breathe"? This book says, you want to feel discouraged, go ahead, feel discouraged. When you get an answer you don't want, how else are you supposed to feel? But here's the thing: Don't let it stop there. Don't sit down and wallow in the discouraging feeling. Keep moving. Slog through it. Come out on the other side of it. It's lighter there. Fresher. The sun is shining.

If I get a discouraging answer today, I'll let my feelings have their way for a while. But I won't sink into them and drown. I'll keep slogging through them. Because I know that on the other side is a better place.

The first Earth Day, held on April 22, 1970, marked a turning point in the history of public understanding of nature and of humankind's place in it.

—*The Environmental Movement*
by Laurence Pringle

Isn't it too bad that we've had to appoint a day to remind us of something that should be as natural as . . . well . . . nature? Kind of like setting aside a day to honor appetite. But understandable, too, because as we humans have changed the face of our planetary home—banishing species to extinction, replacing forests with cities, rerouting rivers—we've come to think of ourselves as *outside of* rather than *within* nature. We forget that as we abuse our environment, we abuse ourselves.

Today I will do what, really, I should do every day—
I will honor the earth. *My* earth.

When they reached the school, Little Brown Bear waved good-bye to Papa Bear and blew Mama Bear a kiss.

—*Little Brown Bear Won't Go to School!*
by Jane Dyer

A father drops his kid off at the mall; the kid bolts from the car to join his friends, never looking back. . . . A mother walks her teenager to school; the teenager walks a block ahead of Mom. . . . Do these scenes sound familiar? Now that you're too big to cling to Mommy and Daddy, do you find it embarrassing to be seen with them? Are they useful for transportation and not much else? Has their place in your life been taken over by your friends?

Do I ignore my parents when other kids are around? Next time my dad drops me off somewhere, I'll say "Thanks, Dad." Next time I'm with my mother and we bump into my friends, I won't act as if I don't know her.

*H*e said practicing every day was more important than how long I practiced.

—*Playing Dad's Song*
by D. Dina Friedman

There's an old story about a farm boy whose father gives him a newborn calf. The boy loves the calf. He is so happy he picks it up and carries it around the barn. He does so the next day, too. And the next. Time passes. The boy becomes a man, the calf becomes a cow, and still, every day: around the barn. When others see the now grown-up farmer carrying a full-grown cow across his shoulders, they marvel: How can this be? And the farmer-once-a-boy simply shrugs and says "We grew up together."

If I wait too long to lift my dream, I may find that it's too heavy. But if I start now, day by day, every day, someday people may marvel at how much I can carry.

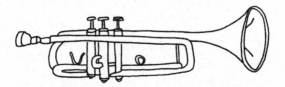

"Sorry, Dewey, but *someone* has to go last. This year it's our turn."

—*Book Fair Day*
by Lynn Plourde
illustrated by Thor Wickstrom

You race to be first in line. You race to get the best seat. You race to be first out of school. We love to be first—and hate to be last. Which is a shame. Because now and then you're going to be last whether you like it or not, so why waste your hate on something you can't avoid? Grow up. Last happens. Deal with it.

If I find myself last in line today, I won't get bent out of shape. Who do I think I am, some Prince of the Universe who never has to be last? Last happens. First happens. It's called life. Big deal.

The whooping cranes take off
like feathered spears.
Once more to northern
nesting grounds they go.
May it always be so.

—*Song for the Whooping Crane*
by Eileen Spinelli and Elsa Warnick

In a world of turmoil and change, we are granted the comfort, the blessing, of those few eternal wonders that stay the same. The turning of the seasons. A parent's love. The annual migrations of humpback whales and whooping cranes. When we are frazzled, it is to such recurring certainties that we reach out and say "Thank you!"

I may never see a whooping crane, but in some small way
it's nice to know that as the elements of my life
come and go, tumble and change, I can always count on that
big white bird heading north year after year after year.
May it always be so.

We're moving today. I'm so scared God. I've never lived anywhere but here.

—*Are You There God? It's Me, Margaret.*
by Judy Blume

New neighborhood. New school. New faces. Change can be scary. And one of the most useless pieces of advice in the world is "Don't be scared." Yeah, right. Easy to say. This book says something else: Hey, go ahead, be scared. It's only natural. Just don't get carried away. And this: Don't be scared while doing nothing. Do stuff. Keep busy. And this: Keep talking. To your family. To your old friends. Even to some of those new, scary faces. Pretty soon you'll find they've become new, not-so-scary friends.

If there's a big change coming, I'll feel free to be scared, but I won't go off the deep end. I'll keep busy and I'll keep talking, and pretty soon I'll feel at home again.

"You tried. All day. With a big heart. And *that's* what counts."

—*The Best Kid in the World*
by Peter H. Reynolds

That *is* what counts. But how can you believe it when so many other voices are braying "YOU GOTTA BE NUMBER ONE!" and "WINNING IS THE ONLY THING THAT COUNTS!"?

Winning is overrated. Starting now, I'll repeat that to myself five times a day until it sinks in. Trophies and medals and blue ribbons are not the only signs of success. I can finish last in a race and still claim a victory that no trophy can express. What really counts is my effort, my heart. No one can truly defeat me without my permission.

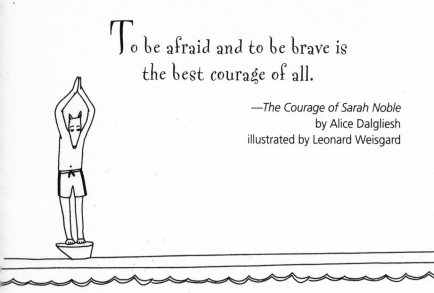

To be afraid and to be brave is
the best courage of all.

—The Courage of Sarah Noble
by Alice Dalgliesh
illustrated by Leonard Weisgard

Fear has value. Oh yes. For without fear there is no bravery. Bravery needs fear like a balloon needs air. Fear gives bravery its shape, makes it soar. We're not talking major fears here, like jumping out of airplanes or swimming with sharks. We're talking little, everyday fears—wearing the "wrong" thing to school, having somebody catch you studying, saying "I love you" to Mom or Dad. Every little fear is an invitation, an opportunity to be brave.

Today I'll do one small brave thing.

Things just are, and fussing don't bring changes.

—*Tuck Everlasting*
by Natalie Babbitt

If you're into poker, you know that the trick is knowing when to hold 'em, knowing when to fold 'em. Sometimes the cards of life fall a stinko way, and, fuss all you want, there's not a thing you can do about it. Except this: Fold 'em with grace and get ready to play the next hand.

Today, if life deals me a bad hand, I won't waste time whining about my rotten luck. I'll just fold 'em and say "Deal 'em again."

D ad bought Jackson
a hamster.
"He's all yours, so
take care of him."

—*Monster Pet!*
by Angela McAllister and Charlotte Middleton

If it hasn't happened already, sooner or later you will be responsible for another person—a child, an aging parent, high school friends in the car you're driving. Will you be ready to meet that responsibility? Have you shown that you can be trusted with another's welfare? Even a hamster's?

Whether it be a pet, a person, or even a plant,
I will accept responsibility for whatever life
is placed in my hands.

Bless chipmunks
and bluebirds and squirrels
raccoons, toucans, tigers
bats and baboons.
Bless barkers and tweeters, quackers
and howlers.

—*Bless This House: A Bedtime Prayer for the World*
by Leslie Staub

Many biologists believe that thirty years from now one-fifth of all species on earth will become extinct. Imagine a world without tigers and sea horses. It could happen—because we humans are proving to be poor neighbors to the other creatures who share this planet with us.

Today I will bless an animal—and resolve to be
as good an earthly neighbor as I can be.

Up cheerup I'm up
Let me be the first to greet the light
First cheerily first
Hello day, good-bye night

—"Robin"
Fireflies at Midnight
by Marilyn Singer
illustrated by Ken Robbins

Birdsong at dawn remains one of life's purest joys. Don't miss it.

Have I ever experienced the simple joy of hearing birds sing before I open my eyes in the morning? Or do I awaken each day to the noise of alarm clocks, TVs, and people-chatter? One of these nights I'll go to bed earlier than usual. I'll leave a window open. At least once in my life, I'm going to wake up to birdsong.

The next morning Mom let me eat
breakfast on the porch. I love eating
outside. Food always tastes
so much better, I think.

—*When Mules Flew on Magnolia Street*
by Angela Johnson

Hey—outdoors! Ever hear of it? You room-dweller. You under-the-roofer. There's the door. Go ahead, take a chance: Step outside. It's not just breakfast—life itself tastes better outside.

Home. School. Car. Mall. Come to think of it,
I'm almost always under a roof. Have I lost touch
with the world outside these walls? I'll open a door,
step outside, get reacquainted.

"It is important for a child to plant
a seed," she [Lady Bird Johnson] told
a friend, "to water it, nourish it,
tend to it, watch it grow. . . ."

—*Miss Lady Bird's Wildflowers: How a First Lady Changed America*
by Kathi Appelt
illustrated by Joy Fisher Hein

You have been nourished, tended. Your growing up has been carefully watched. To cultivate a seed is to care for, to cherish new life, to echo the attention that you yourself have received. To grow a plant is to anticipate that day when it will be more than seeds that you will tend.

Today I will keep looking until I find, somewhere,
a sign of new life.

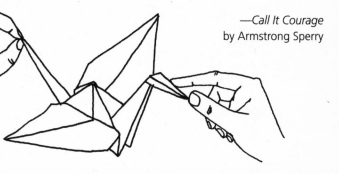

He was quick and clever with his hands, and now he was grateful for the skill which was his.

—*Call It Courage*
by Armstrong Sperry

We live in a world in which manual labor is widely devalued. Fame and money set the standard of the ambitious. Few discover the simple, ancient satisfaction of working with one's hands. Something deep in the human soul is fulfilled when sanding a piece of homemade furniture or shaping silver and gems into a sun-spangled dragonfly.

I'm going to make something. Maybe I'll get ideas from a book or a crafts fair. Maybe I'll make an origami bird, with nothing but a piece of paper. If it turns out well, I'll give it to someone.

A is for Asparagus.

—*The Vegetable Alphabet Book*
by Jerry Pallotta and Bob Thomson
illustrated by Edgar Stewart

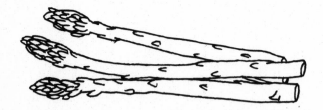

If you eat all your vegetables, skip this page and take the day off. If not . . .

I can't! I can't! I can't! I can't eat that green thing because it doesn't taste like ice cream. Please don't make me. I'll cry. See? Real tears. Boohoo. And don't tell me for the billionth time "They're good for you." OK, listen, I'll do it just for the one day. Not because you said so and not because they're good for me. I'll do it because I'm reading this book and I trust it and the last thing it says on this page is . . .

TODAY I WILL EAT A VEGETABLE.

Ẅith the food went
polite conversation.

So how was
your day today?

—*Saffy's Angel*
by Hilary McKay

McDonald's, picnic, fancy banquet—wherever people gather to dine, there's more than eating going on. There's talk. It's a good idea to keep the talk pleasant. Leave the hassles and hard knocks for other times. Let good talk be the side dish with every meal. It's good for your well-being—and your digestion.

I won't spoil my meals with arguments
and contentious talk. I'll keep it light, positive, pleasant.
When my stomach is happy, I'm happy.

*T*here once was a man
who danced in the street.

—*Rap A Tap Tap*
by Leo and Diane Dillon

If he danced in the street, you can be sure he'd also be happy to dance on the beach, in the parking lot, in the mall, on the roof. This is a guy with an urge for exuberant expression that predates the constraints of civilization. The lesson here: When the spirit moves you to dance—*dance!*

Am I wound too tight? Overcivilized? Do I schedule my fun? Dance only on a dance floor? Next time I feel like dancing, I'll dance—even if I'm in a parking lot.

When someone else is talking,
you should be quiet
until they're finished.
Even if they talk a very long time.

—*Please Is a Good Word to Say*
by Barbara Joosse
illustrated by Jennifer Plecas

If someone asked you "What is conversation?" you might well answer "It's two or more people talking to each other." Or would you say "It's two or more people listening to each other"? Speaking is only half of communication; listening is the other half. Listening skills are just as important as speaking skills.

Sure, I listen—but exactly whom am I listening to? Am I so busy listening to myself that I'm not really hearing what others say? Today I'll concentrate on listening to the other person—and maybe find out what I've been missing.

Minds, like diapers, need occasional changing.

—*The Ballad of Lucy Whipple*
by Karen Cushman

People who change their minds all the time are called in-decisive, wishy-washy. People who never change their minds are called rigid, stubborn. Strive to be somewhere in the middle. The human mind is a constantly changing thing. It's never quite the same two days in a row. Your mind is there to inform you, to serve you. Be a partner with your mind, not a dictator.

I have an opinion today, but twenty-four hours
from now my mind may have collected new information.
I will not muzzle my mind with stubbornness.
I will give it a chance to be heard.

But then I looked and soon I saw,
That scarecrow was all stuffed with straw!

—"Scarecrow Eyes"
Shout! Little Poems that Roar
by Brod Bagert
illustrated by Sachiko Yoshikawa

Life is populated with scarecrows—all those people and things that seem so scary and trouble our sleep. Isn't it nice to know that most of them turn out to be made of nothing but straw?

A bully. A new school. A stern teacher. A tryout. Hardly a day passes when I don't have to confront at least one scarecrow. But, hey, I'm a person, not a crow, and I know that the best way to deal with a scarecrow is not to fly away but to meet it head-on.

... I'll bring your gifts—
ribbons for your branches,
buckets of water, and
a wheelbarrow of mulch.

—"Celebration"
Old Elm Speaks: Tree Poems
by Kristine O'Connell George
illustrated by Kate Kiesler

Isn't this a nice idea? Nature gives us so much. Why not give something back?

From day's dawning to spectacular sunset, I am daily the receiver of nature's gifts. Today I'll be the giver. I'll tie a ribbon to my favorite tree or plant.

"She started it," Jack said.

—*The Rudest Alien on Earth*
by Jane Leslie Conly

We've all been Jacks at one time or another, justifying our bad behavior by pointing to someone else and saying "*He* started it!" . . . "*She* started it!" When someone does something really nice, are we just as quick to follow suit and point and say "*She* started it"?

No more passing the buck. If someone tries to goad me into bad behavior, I'll either be mature enough not to get sucked in or, if I do participate, mature enough to take the heat myself.

YOU

The only thing that keeps my spirits
buoyed is this letter I received
from Daniel.

*—A Light in the Storm: The Civil War Diary of Amelia Martin,
Fenwick Island, Delaware, 1861* (Dear America series)
by Karen Hesse

We seem to live in a world of big gestures. Skywritten marriage proposals. Extravagant birthday parties. The more expensive the gift, the more it counts. Size and price tags may dazzle the eye, but the heart—the heart is touched by sincerity.

Is there someone in my life whose spirit needs picking up? As I consider how to respond, I'll think small, not big; real, not expensive.

[Big Anthony] was so busy listening to compliments from everyone that he didn't notice the pasta pot was still bubbling and boiling. . . .

—*Strega Nona*
by Tomie de Paola

Who doesn't love a compliment? But every compliment comes with a warning: Beware—Do Not Overuse. Go ahead, sniff your compliment. Take a little sip. But don't chew, don't swallow. If you do, you risk abandoning the good work that inspired the compliment in the first place. If that happens, maybe it was the compliment and not the job well done that you were aiming for all along.

Every day I work at stuff. Sometimes I try really hard. Today I'll ask myself this question: Exactly *why* am I trying hard? Is it because I want to do a good job? Or because I'm fishing for compliments?

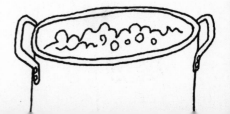

F or my mother's sake I would
keep an eye on my sister.

—*Shark Bite*
by Todd Strasser

"For my mother's sake." How many good deeds in this
world might never happen without a "mother's sake" to
provoke them? When uncertainty or just plain laziness
leaves you as inactive as a rock, that's a good time to check
in with the world's greatest motivator.

This happens a lot: There's something I know ought to be
done, but I'm not doing it because no one has told me to.
If it happens today, I'll ask myself "Will Mom be happy
if I do it?" And follow the answer.

Mend-It McGregor, everyone called him, because he could mend most anything that needed mending. . . .

—*Inventor McGregor*
by Kathleen T. Pelley
illustrated by Michael Chesworth

This is not a mend-it age we live in. We are obsessed with the brand-new. If it's broken, worn, dirty, used, old—toss it. Even cameras are disposable. It's an unfortunate mind-set, in view of our planet's disappearing resources. What we need is a return to the mend-it mentality. We need to relearn a basic truth of economics: It's usually cheaper to fix something than to replace it.

Have I thrown out anything lately that could have been fixed? From now on, I'll take a second look at stuff before I toss it.

I forgot to tell you in the last letter
three important things that I'm
too shy to say to your face.

—*The Gardener*
by Sarah Stewart
illustrated by David Small

Regret is a hard thing to live with. Especially hard is the regret of words unsaid. Regretful and unnecessary—for there are ways to work around shyness.

Is there something I've been wanting to say to someone but I'm too shy to say it in person? If so, I'll write it out today. And tomorrow, if my words still feel right, I'll deliver them.

I'm tired out from telling people
what not to do.

—*No Laughing, No Smiling, No Giggling*
by James Stevenson

Does it sometimes seem as if there are only about three things in the universe that you're allowed to do? That you're surrounded by all these DON'T people (parents, teachers, coaches)? DON'T this, DON'T that. Here's the bad news: It's not going to change. But be honest, now—a lot of that stuff you didn't even *want* to do until the word *don't* was stuck in front of it, right? So here's the ticket: Concentrate on DOING, not DON'TING. You'll be so busy DOING good stuff, they'll have to go find somebody else to say DON'T to.

Today I'll concentrate on DO, not DON'T.

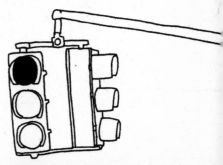

"Gecko," said Elephant. "This world is all connected. Some things you just have to put up with."

—*Go to Sleep, Gecko! A Balinese Folktale*
retold by Margaret Read MacDonald
illustrated by Geraldo Valério

Since the word *ecology* (look it up if you don't know it) became popular a few decades ago, the idea that everything is interconnected and interdependent is no longer big news. Which is a shame. This is what happens when a terrific, insightful idea gets tagged with an overused word. We don't stop to ask: What's a wasp got to do with me?

If I were going to go corny on this subject, I might stop at the next worm I see and say "Greetings, brother!" Or, more seriously, I might take five minutes out of this day and look around myself and try, just try, to grasp the idea that I am connected to everything and everything is connected to me.

"Hi, sleepyhead," she said. "You've been
missing a lot of pretty countryside. . . .
It's been like something out of
a picture book."
"Has it?" Kit said with disinterest.

—*Down a Dark Hall*
by Lois Duncan

Parent tries to start pleasant conversation with her kid. Kid
couldn't care less. Sound familiar?

Do my parents try to maintain contact with me in simple
ways I couldn't care less about? Does it ever occur to me
that when they make dumb remarks, they really don't care
what I say in reply? They just want to hear my voice.
If such a remark comes my way today, I'll respond with
some warmth and actual words. I'll give grunts and short,
flat answers the day off.

"Forever and always," I said, "no matter what happens, we'll be best friends."

—*Stepping on the Cracks*
by Mary Downing Hahn

Here's how it goes with many people: The older they get, the less they use the word *forever*. Some grizzled grown-ups become downright cynical and practically sneer whenever they hear the word. These people miss an important point: The joyful abandon and just plain humanness of leapfrogging from today to Forever for the sake of anything from a friend to cotton candy.

I wonder if I'll use the word *forever* today. If I feel it coming on, I won't stop it; I'll let it out. I understand that many Forevers in fact don't last forever. Big deal. I'll express how I feel now and let Forever take care of itself.

When Flying Jack was four years old,
people would ask, "What do you want
to be when you grow up?"
"A pilot!" he would say.

—*Flying Jack*
by Kathye Fetsko Petrie
illustrated by Paula J. Mahoney

Flying Jack, a fictional character based on the author's father, did become a pilot—fifty-six years later. What took him so long? Something called life got in the way. *Having* a dream and *working toward* a dream are usually good things. *Becoming* a dream at the expense of all else is usually not such a good thing. Jack is not willing to sacrifice his family for his dream, and his wife and seven children are eternally grateful for that. So grateful that, on his sixtieth birthday, they give him the thing he's always dreamed of: flying lessons.

I will be a responsible dreamer. I will feel free to have my
dreams and to work toward them, but I will keep them in
perspective. I will not allow them to run my whole life.
I will not forfeit my self for my dreams.

"I'm sure you're much nicer
than you look!"

—*Pollyanna*
by Eleanor H. Porter

Look at the faces on a crowded sidewalk and you might conclude that humanity is nothing but grumps and grouches. You've been told not to judge a book by its cover (not even this one); neither should you judge people by *their* covers—that is, their appearance. One of the sweetest delights of human experience is discovering that someone is actually much nicer than he or she appears to be.

I will try to live this whole day without judging people by their covers. I will not assume that a grumpy face equals a grumpy person.

When something frightening happens, the best thing to do, I think, is to stay calm, figure out what to do, and then (even if you're afraid) make yourself do it, no matter what.

—*Blow Out the Moon*
by Libby Koponen

That thing inside your skull, between your ears and behind your eyes: your brain. Ring a bell? It performs quite a few jobs for you, but maybe the most important of all is this: *It thinks*. So use it. Especially if you're scared or in a tight spot. Let it size up the situation and figure out the best way to deal with it. Then go—follow your brain's advice.

If I get scared today, I won't panic. I'll use my head. It's good to know I have help ready and waiting between my ears.

Rachel was mindful of her mother's sacrifices and grateful for her support.

—*Up Close: Rachel Carson*
by Ellen Levine

With the publication of Rachel Carson's famous book *The Sea Around Us*, people began to appreciate the natural blessings of our planet. Perhaps it's not surprising that Rachel Carson began by appreciating the blessings of her own mother. We could all do worse than follow Rachel Carson's example.

Do I take my mother for granted? Do I appreciate her sacrifice and support? Or do I figure "Hey, what's the big deal? She's only doing her job." Or don't I even notice? Starting today, I'm going to notice. Starting today, I'll take a dusty old word off the shelf and put it to use.

The word is *gratitude*.

Tomorrow: Dad's turn.

Grandpa says, "It's all right, Jessica. All artists make mistakes. And sometimes you can turn a mistake into something good."

—*Lunchtime for a Purple Snake*
by Harriet Zeifert
illustrated by Todd McKie

Of course, it's not only artists who make mistakes—we all do. Every day. And yet we treat mistakes as if they were poison. When NASA sends a space probe to a distant planet, the engineers know their aim will not be perfect. Once they determine exactly how imperfect it is, they send out signals for a midcourse correction. In other words, their mistake helps steer them to their target. Get the point?

I get the point. If I make a mistake today, I won't get down on myself or treat it like the end of the world. I'll use it as a midcourse correction and continue toward my goal.

And you greet the village chief respectfully.
"Jambo, Mzee!" Hello, Respected One!

—*For You Are a Kenyan Child*
by Kelly Cunnane
illustrated by Ana Juan

"Respect your elders." It was once a widespread rule of life. Kids used to hear it all the time. "Respect your elders." Do they still? Do you? Respect is the oil that makes the machinery of society run smoothly.

My elders have already been down the road of years that I have yet to travel. Just for that, they deserve my respect.

*H*er smile was like a big, warm hug.

—*The Day Eddie Met the Author*
by Louise Borden
illustrated by Adam Gustavson

Sometimes a smile is like other things, too. A cozy blanket. A fond reminder of good times. An affirmation of friendship. Welcome to a stranger. Comfort to the fearful. Or a sign that says I UNDERSTAND.

Today I will give someone my best smile. I'll aim it at
a person who probably doesn't expect it from me.
As for the particular effect my smile may produce,
I'll leave that up to the target.

Finally, the end of the month arrived.
"It's time to unlock your banks,"
Mrs. O'Malley announced.

—*Willie Wins*
by Almira Astudillo Gilles
illustrated by Carl Angel

Is there a Mrs. O'Malley in your house? Someone who helps you to manage your money? Someone who tells you that money doesn't rot, so you don't *have* to spend it the first minute you get it—or even the first week? Someone who tells you that if you save your money, an amazing thing happens—it grows!

Is there someone in my house to help me manage my money?
If so, I'll appoint him or her my Mrs. O'Malley.
If not, I'll appoint myself.

[Chester Cricket] began to chirp to ease
his feelings. He found that it helped
somehow if you sang your sadness.

—*The Cricket in Times Square*
by George Selden
illustrated by Garth Williams

Tears or sullen silence or lashing out are not the only ways
to cope with sadness. Some sad feelings crave a voice, even
a song. That's what "singin' the blues" is all about.

Will sadness visit me today? How will I respond? Maybe
I'll try something I've never done before. Maybe I'll find
myself a solitary place and quietly hum my sadness. Or—
what the heck—maybe just belt it out. If it helps, I won't
ask why. If it works, it works. Hey, if it's good enough
for Chester Cricket . . .

Tom had hoped today would be
as ordinary as possible.

—*The Boy Who Saved Baseball*
by John H. Ritter

BOR-ing.

How many kids use this word to describe their hometown? their school? their life? Those kids should be reminded of an old Chinese curse: "May you live in interesting times." The author of the curse knew that interesting times are often interesting in ways that make us long for the good old boring ordinary days. Better to find the positives in ordinary times because:

1. Most times are, by definition, ordinary, so you might as well make the best of them.

2. You might not like the alternative.

Today may be ordinary, but that doesn't mean it has to be
boring, not if I find the *extraordinary* within it.
And, anyway, who am I to blame the day?
Is it the day that's boring—or me?

"I know I don't need a dog.
But this dog needs me."

—*Because of Winn-Dixie*
by Kate DiCamillo

"I want! I want! I want!" These words pretty much describe infancy, even little-kidhood. You have taken a step toward grown-uphood when it occurs to you that others have wants and needs, too. And an even bigger step when it occurs to you that you yourself can be the answer to those needs.

I've spent enough of my life telling the world what I want, what I need. As of now, I'm shifting the focus to what others need. In fact, today I'll make it a point to identify at least one fellow creature (human or otherwise) with a need that I can answer.

When I had some trouble I wrote to my grandma about it.

—*My Grandma, My Pen Pal*
by Jan Dale Koutsky

When you're having trouble, you say you don't think of telling your grandma or grandpa. Big mistake. You don't get to be a grandparent without scaling a Mt. Everest of troubles. Listen to Grandma—she can tell you where the handholds are.

Today I'll give Grandma or Grandpa a call.

Dear Grandma,
How are you? I
am writing because
I have some trouble
...ted your

"You're not the boss of me,"
said Skippyjon Jones.
"In your dreams . . ." said Mama.

—*Skippyjon Jones in the Dog-House*
by Judy Schachner

Let's be real. Being a kid day in and day out is a big enough job. Why pile Boss on top of it? Your parents have already volunteered for the job. Let them have it.

The only way I'm ever going to be Total Absolute #1 Boss of Myself is if I live alone. And let's face it—even though I sometimes act as if I want to live alone, I really don't.

When you're feeling sorry for yourself,
everything looks beige and gray.

—*Throwing Shadows*
by E. L. Konigsburg

That's the thing about self-pity—it doesn't stay with the
self. It spreads out until it covers and colors everything.
You're just one person, yet your mood has the power to
affect the whole world. Makes you wonder, doesn't it—if
you're so doggone powerful, why are you feeling sorry for
yourself in the first place?

If I feel like feeling sorry for myself today, I won't.

Advice from friends is like
the weather. Some of it is good;
some of it is bad.

—"The Baboon's Umbrella"
Fables
by Arnold Lobel

Hey, it's one thing to listen to your friends' advice, another thing to follow it. So listen all you want. But before following, check with your favorite grown-up.

Today I'll be careful not to believe everything I hear.

"*H*e's been through a lot, and he deserves some consideration."

—*Belle Prater's Boy*
by Ruth White

It is a distinctive feature of the human being—one that separates us from eels and beetles (but maybe not elephants)—that we have interpersonal sensitivity. That is, the ability to be aware of what another person is going through, whether it be a good time or a bad time. And not only to be aware of it but to treat that person accordingly. This is human behavior at its best.

Sure, I'm aware of how *I* feel. Every minute of every day. But am I aware of how *others* feel? What are *they* going through? Are *they* having a good or bad day? Am I sensitive enough to sympathize or celebrate with them? Am I separating myself from eels and beetles?

"Mom and Dad and the Pinks have been lost at sea," she cried out.

—"Love"
Jack's New Power: Stories from a Caribbean Year
by Jack Gantos

Literature—and, unfortunately, life—is filled with tragic announcements like this. In life, they almost always take us by surprise. In most cases there's little or nothing we can do to avoid them. But there is one thing we can do: We can appreciate what we do have—today, this minute.

I hope I never hear words like those above. But I know it's possible, and because of that I'm going to give each member of my family a hug today.

... She heard the *slap-slap* of drying laundry; the *flap-flap* of pigeon wings; the *jing-aling-ling* of lire; and the *ting-aling-ling* of church bells.

—*Gabriella's Song*
by Candace Fleming
illustrated by Giselle Potter

You hear the music you like, and you hear the voices of your friends and parents and teachers—and yourself—but other than that, do you really hear the sounds of the world around you? So much goes unnoticed because we squeeze our senses into narrow, habitual channels.

Wouldn't it be a shame to live my whole life without ever hearing the sound of a bird's wings or the buzz of a bee? Today I'm going to go somewhere outside and stand alone and close my eyes and tune out the usual stuff and for once just listen—*listen*—to the world around me.

Jack forgot very little of what he saw.

—*The Sea of Trolls*
by Nancy Farmer

Good for Jack. Most of us aren't so lucky. You disagree? Name the wall color of every room in your house. What's the color of the floors in your school's hallways? The human memory fails to retain much of what it encounters. Unless you hope to become a spy or a writer, it's probably not important that you improve greatly in this area. What is important is this: Before you swear that you saw something—especially if that something might be hurtful to someone—bite your lip and remember how imperfect is the human memory.

I have a flaw common to all people except for total-recall Jacks: I routinely forget most of what I see. I'll remember this—I swear—and take it into account before talking about others.

In spite of everything I still believe that people are really good at heart.

—*Anne Frank: The Diary of a Young Girl*
by Anne Frank

Wow! If Anne Frank, stuck in the middle of the Holocaust, could say that, who are we *not* to say it? And, really, would you want it any other way? Remember—you, too, are a "people." If people are basically rotten, what does that say about you? Much better to belong to a species that is basically good guys, right?

I'm thinking of a kid who gives people a bad name. I'm going to remind myself that there is good in all people, and before I go to bed tonight, I'm going to find it in this kid.

"You always tell me that I never ask for help when I need it, Michael. I'm asking now."

—*Sand Dollar Summer*
by Kimberly K. Jones

It's no disgrace to ask for help. In fact, to never ask for help is foolish. Every "self-sufficient" person has received help along the way.

Next time I need help,
I'll ask for it.

"I don't believe I've eaten strawberries before," said Claudius.

—*Thimbleberry Stories*
by Cynthia Rylant
illustrated by Maggie Kneen

Claudius is talking about food, but the point can be expanded: Don't be afraid to try new things. There may be no more continents to discover, but nothing is stopping you from discovering the taste of a new fruit.

Is my life a trench-work of habits? Do I plod along the same deep ruts day after day? Today I'll climb out of my usual self and try something new—whether it's listening to a new kind of music, or tasting something I've never tried before, or even a simple little thing like laughing out loud or saying "Hi" to someone who doesn't expect it.

She surprised her friend David because when they wrestled she could toss him halfway across the Wick kitchen two out of three times.

—*This Time, Tempe Wick?*
by Patricia Lee Gauch
illustrated by Margot Tomes

So why is David "surprised"? Because girls aren't *supposed* to be able to outwrestle boys two-thirds of the time? If David is smart, he'll realize he's landed smack in the middle of a lesson in life: Beware of stuff you suppose. Especially when it comes to girls vs. boys. If you're a boy, don't underestimate girls. If you're a girl, don't underestimate yourself.

How many things do I suppose about the opposite sex that in fact are not true? Sure, there are bodily differences. Sure, guys are often better at some things, girls at others. But there are too many exceptions to make a rule. So let the rule be, simply, this: Girls = Boys.

But I thought brave thoughts to comfort me.

—The Bravest of the Brave
by Shutta Crum
illustrated by Tim Bowers

At one time or another everyone is afraid. What counts is how we handle our fear, how we deal with fearful situations. One way is to think brave thoughts. This makes a lot of sense, because the body often follows the brain. As the popular saying goes: You are what you think.

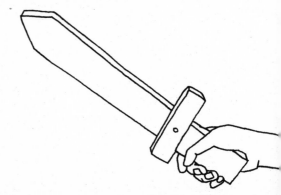

Next time I'm in a fearful situation, I'll picture myself being brave. Thinking so will help me to become so.

Susan made her office a warm and welcoming place.

—*Native American Doctor: The Story of Susan LaFlesche Picotte*
by Jeri Ferris

You're probably too young to have an office, but how about your room or the den or the basement—wherever it is that you have friends over? Is it "warm and welcoming"? Is it an extension of yourself? Does it bring a smile to a visitor's face just to walk in? Does it say "Make yourself at home. *My* space is *your* space"?

Today I'll try to look at my space through the eyes of a visitor. If it doesn't feel warm and welcoming, I'll do something about it.

E ach mussel
somehow finds a rock to cling to,
opening when washed by water,
closing when the tide goes out.

—"Mussels"
The Braid
by Helen Frost

Not all beautiful things come in gaudy colors, announcing themselves with fanfare and fancy display. If you can see beauty in an abandoned cicada shell or in the cocked head of a robin looking for worms or in the miracle of a tide-water mussel—that is to say, if something inside you thrills to the sight of the world simply being itself—beauty will always find you.

There's no need to wait for a glorious sunset or visit a museum. I walk through beauty every day—from the scurry of ants to the nighttime sky—the beauty of this wonderful, endlessly fascinating universe simply being itself. Have I been paying attention? Today I will.

As it was a car meant for four,
and there were five passengers, there was
no seat belt for Nick.

—*Everlost*
by Neal Shusterman

One of the things kids are most famous for is this: They think they're going to live forever. The number of deaths each year due to unbuckled seat belts says otherwise.

Do I think I'm going to live forever? Would I get into a car that has only four seat belts if I were the fifth person? Am I *stupid*?

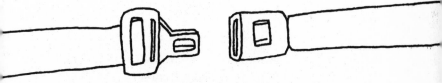

If you ever met Mum, it's that hug you'd remember.

—The Wedding Planner's Daughter
by Coleen Murtagh Paratore

How will people remember you? Everyone you meet carries away a memory of you. Something you said. Something you did. Day after day, year after year. A lifetime of personal monuments in the memories of others.

Knowing that my words and actions are registered in the memories of others reminds me that my life is being memorialized even as I live it day by day. Today I will make sure those memories are good ones.

"The little birds sang as if it were
The one day of summer in all the year."

—*Anne of Green Gables*
by L. M. Montgomery

Oh, to live in a world of one-and-only days! How much more we would appreciate the treasure of each passing moment. Sing, little bird, sing—for you and not the sun alone make the summer shine.

Today I rejoice in this, the First Day of Summer!

I especially like to write when I'm bored, because then I'm not anymore.

—Author: A True Story
by Helen Lester

We're not just talking stories. Any kind of writing will do. Poem. Article. Joke. Letter (to friend, grandparent, uncle, aunt, teacher, cousin, editor, president, queen of England, favorite author, your dog, etc.). List (New Year's resolutions, favorite things, favorite people, least favorite people, ten wishes, ten fears, ten delights, etc.). Diary. Journal. Greeting card. Backyard stage play. Living room comedy show. Thank-you note. Secret confession. See? Just reading this list of things you can write made you forget you were bored.

If I get bored today, I'll pick something from the list above and de-bore myself.

Once upon a

The only good reason for swimming as far as I can see is to escape drowning.

—*Ordinary Jack*
by Helen Cresswell

Well, as a reason for learning to swim, that's OK for starters. But there are other reasons, too: stay healthy; cool off on hot days; meet other girls or boys; meet fish. And something metaphysical: a return to the environment that spawned life on earth itself.

If I haven't done so already, today I make this vow:
I will learn to swim.

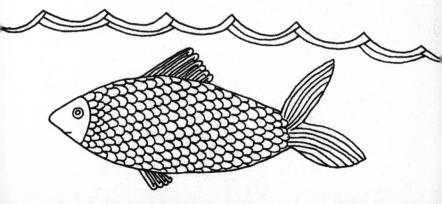

We hear all the music
that's in the wind.

—*A Day No Pigs Would Die*
by Robert Newton Peck

Do you believe that the only way to hear music is at a concert or through headphones or on the radio? Sure, there are guitars and pianos, but music comes from many other "instruments" as well: the mutter of rain on a roof, the babble of stream water, the laughter of children, the symphony of insects on a summer's night, the sound of wind in the trees. Take off your headphones. *Listen*.

There is music all around me, and it's not all coming from
speakers and iPods. Today I'll listen.

Now maybe there was only one way left for her to try to help Jim. To chase that awful look out of his eyes and get him to talk again. That would be worth a really *big* sacrifice.

—*Keeping Score*
by Linda Sue Park

Jim is a grown-up, shell-shocked from his exposure to war. Maggie is just a kid. Yet Maggie does something that we usually associate with grown-ups rather than kids. She makes a sacrifice. She stops rooting for her beloved Brooklyn Dodgers. She roots instead for the New York Giants—because the Giants are Jim's favorite team.

Sacrifice. It's not a word I usually associate with myself. I know that my parents and others in my life make sacrifices for me (although, frankly, I spend too little time appreciating it). But who says I, too, can't do some sacrificing now and then? Is it possible that the only thing standing between a friend and happiness is my willingness to give up something? Sacrifice—a powerful force, and it's all mine.

"I'll win as many medals,"
She said when just a kid,
"As anyone who ever lived."
And that's just what she did.

—"First Lady of Sports"
by J. Patrick Lewis
(from *More Spice Than Sugar: Poems About Feisty Females*,
compiled by Lillian Morrison, illustrated by Ann Boyajian)

The "she" in the verse is "Babe" Didrikson Zaharias. As a little girl, Babe could outrun, outjump, and outthrow the boys. She grew up to become what many consider the greatest female athlete of all time. She proved to everyone that when it comes to sports, girls can do more than lead the cheers.

Do I think playing sports is for boys, cheering is for girls?
Today I'll think again.

We got to stick together like mornin' glories stick on a picket fence.

—*Be Ever Hopeful, Hannalee*
by Patricia Beatty

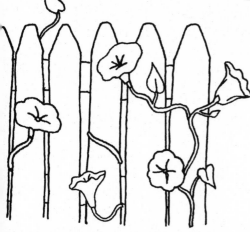

Sometimes people are like trees—we stand straight, tall, alone. Sometimes we're more like morning glory vines—we need support or we fall. And sometimes it's knowing which we need to be that day—tree or morning glory—that makes all the difference.

Will I be a tree today? Or a morning glory? Whichever—I'm thankful I can be either.

Wear a wide-brimmed hat when you're out in the sun!

—Antarctic Journal: Four Months at the Bottom of the World
by Jennifer Owings Dewey

OK, so you're not at the South Pole and you don't own a wide-brimmed hat, and even if you did, you wouldn't wear it. The point is, it's summer, and that means sunny days, and that means this reminder is due: Too much sun is bad for you. Limit your exposure. Years from now your cancer-free, wrinkle-free skin will thank you.

Older generations didn't know about the dangers of too much sun. I do—thanks to my parents, doctors, and commercials for sunblock. Sure, I love summer and I love sun. But when the sun is highest and hottest, I'll stay cool—and live longer—in the shade.

I make customized birdhouses.

—*Jobs for Kids*
by Jeanne Kiefer
illustrated by Carol Nicklaus

How long do you want your parents to keep paying for everything? (Hah—don't answer that.) But, seriously, the money faucet will not flow forever. Sooner or later you'll have to make your own. Now, let's be clear—this book recommends that you pour most of your efforts into school and healthy activities and volunteering. But if you have an itch to do something more productive with a few of those spare minutes that you now spend with your computer or TV or cell phone, think about the look on your parents' faces when you tell them "I just got a job!" or "I'm going into business for myself!"

Do I spend all my spare time in the company of TVs, computers, and cell phones? Might I be doing something that would give me more satisfaction, plus extra money to boot? And the look on my parents' faces? Priceless!

Officer Buckle knew more safety tips
than anyone else in Napville.

—*Officer Buckle and Gloria*
by Peggy Rathman

You're already learning that it can be a dangerous world out there. Traffic. Strangers. Germs. For years you've been getting safety tips from the Officer Buckles in your life. Now it's time to play Officer Buckle yourself.

Today I'll make a list of at least five safety tips—tips that
I've figured out for myself. Then I'll share them
with some little kids.

Most people, they have only ever seen the movie. But me, I read the book.

—*Harry Sue*
by Sue Stauffacher

This may come as a shocker: The book is usually better than the movie. No kidding.

Next time I have a choice of reading the book or watching the movie, I won't make a choice at all. I'll do both—and see if the foregoing shocker is true.

"This man was my father, your great-grandfather. He was a shepherd."

—*Benito's Bizcochitos*
by Ana Baca
illustrated by Anthony Accardo

BAA

There is more to your family than the people living in your house. Your family extends back into the past, down the line of your ancestors. Get to know them. Ask your parents and grandparents and great-grandparents about *their* grandparents. This is history you won't find in books.

I want to know more about my own family. Next chance I get, I'll ask my oldest living relative to tell me about family members I'll never meet in person.

Some wild boys set off firecrackers.

—Lucy's Summer
by Donald Hall
illustrated by Michael McCurdy

Set off firecrackers and never gave a thought to consequences. Kids do a lot of things without considering consequences: from eating too much candy (lose lunch) to firecrackers (lose a finger) to drugs (lose a future) to driving too fast (lose a life). You will pass one of maturity's milestones on the day you understand—truly understand—that there is such a thing as tomorrow and that *that's* when you will have to live with the consequences of today.

I will think about *consequences* until it becomes more than just an empty word. When I turn this page to tomorrow's page, I will do so with a full set of fingers.

What led up to the Declaration of Independence? And why was this document so important that each year we celebrate the day it was adopted?

—*Fireworks, Picnics, and Flags: The Story of the Fourth of July Symbols*
by James Cross Giblin
illustrated by Ursula Arndt

When you think of the Fourth of July, what comes to mind? Fireworks, picnics, and parades? Or Bunker Hill, Nathan Hale, and "When in the course of human events . . ."? By now there have been hundreds of Fourths of July. All of them—and the nature of the life you live today—were created by the first. You should think about that, too.

Today I'll enjoy the holiday. I'll celebrate. But that's not all. I'll also remember exactly what it is that I'm celebrating.

"There's a tree in it, but it isn't about trees. It's about this girl, Francie, who's poor and doesn't have any money, but it doesn't stop her from doing what she wants to do."

—*A Boy No More*
by Harry Mazer

Francie is the main character in *A Tree Grows in Brooklyn*. She teaches us all that we can be rich in life even if we're not rich in money. The riches of human life—experiences, relationships, the passing parade of days, the simple miracle of waking each morning to the risen sun—it's all there, free for the taking. There's more to life than shopping.

There's more to life than shopping.
There's more to life than shopping.
There's more to life than shopping.

"I want a road!" he cried.
"A road?" said the mayor.

—*From Here to There*
by Nancy Skultety
illustrated by Tammie Lyon

Note the mayor's response. Like this is news to him. The point here is that when it comes to community improvements or many other things in this world, little gets done until someone—or a herd of someones—stands up and says "I want . . ."

Is there something that would make my neighborhood better? Safer? Are we all just waiting around for somebody else to come along and do it? Or does somebody need to stand up and tell the people in charge "We want!" Could that someone be me?

Monday afternoon Wendell Fultz's mother told him to clean his room. "It's turning into a pigsty," she said.

—Pigsty
by Mark Teague

Is your room a pigsty? Unfit for human habitation? Are you such a Hall of Fame slob that you wouldn't know a pigsty if you lived in one? Wendell Fultz comes home one day to discover that his mother's words have come true: He's sharing his room with pigs! At first he thinks it's pretty cool. And then he doesn't—and he gets a taste of what it's like for his family to live with a pigsty kid.

If my parents' room were a pigsty, how would I like it? Sure, my room is my room, but does that give me the right to be disgusting? If my room is making a statement about me, does that statement have to be *Yeccccch*? I'll clean up my act.

Jeremy swallowed. He didn't really
believe the thing upstairs was an egg.
But . . . Tonight he would try
to hatch a dragon.

—*Jeremy Thatcher, Dragon Hatcher*
by Bruce Coville
illustrated by Gary A. Lippincott

At least once in a lifetime, everyone should try to hatch a dragon. In every life there's a "thing upstairs," a possibility that may be (a) mysterious, (b) scary, (c) impossible, (d) not believed in. Walking up those dark stairs and hatching that impossible possibility may turn out to be the best thing you ever do. Dragon eggs await.

Is there a dragon egg in my attic? Am I curious enough to
find out? Bold enough to ascend the dark stairs?

Never tease a weasel.

—*Never Tease a Weasel*
by Jean Conder Soule
illustrated by George Booth

Or a dog or cat or any other animal—at least, not in a mean-spirited way. Playful teasing of a pet is one thing, but teasing that frustrates or angers has no place in a human-animal relationship.

Mean teasing of pets—be they mine or my friends'—is hereby off-limits. And that goes for weasels, too.

Right now, you're doing what for Frederick Douglass was an illegal activity that enabled him to become a free man. You are reading.

—*50 American Heroes Every Kid Should Meet*
by Dennis Denenberg and Lorraine Roscoe

Hard to believe there was a time when reading was against the law in this country. But it's true—if you were a slave. The white masters who made the law were neither crazy nor stupid. They knew perfectly well that knowledge frees the spirit. It wasn't chains of iron that Frederick Douglass broke out of—it was chains of ignorance.

The ability to read and the simple freedom to do so are things I take for granted. (For sure, I would value reading more if it were against the law.) Today I'll take a moment to salute this underappreciated part of my life.

I remember when a rock star . . . put on a huge concert called Live Aid to help people. . . . But he was famous. Could I make a difference too?

—*Peace One Day: The Making of World Peace Day*
by Jeremy Gilley and Karen Blessen

Yes.

Too often we measure ourselves against celebrities and headlines. There are two main ways you can help. You can help someone in your local little world (run errands for a neighbor, bake cookies for someone sick). And you can make money (lemonade stand, yard sale) and send the proceeds to a charity that benefits the larger, global world.

So, again: YES!

I'll start planning today.

JULY 12
(PABLO NERUDA'S BIRTHDAY)

*H*e was too shy to ask the price.

—*To Go Singing through the World:
The Childhood of Pablo Neruda*
by Deborah Kogan Ray

Long before he became a great poet, little Pablo Neruda had something in common with kids the world over: He clammed up in the presence of adults. It's a shame kids don't realize that one of the most impressive things they can do is simply look a grown-up in the eye and speak.

If I opened a door and found myself in a room full of adults, I'd turn right around and walk out. I admit I'm more comfortable with kids than adults. On the other hand, I'm not stupid. I understand that the human race consists of grown-ups, too, and if I'm going to get along in this world, I'd better learn to talk to them. I'll start today.

$6

If I waited for a bus with my mother . . . she would light a cigarette, and a bus would come almost immediately.

—*Sing a Song of Tuna Fish*
by Esmé Raji Codell
illustrated by LeUyen Pham

And so, having barely begun to puff, the narrator's mother stomps out the cigarette and climbs aboard the bus. Even buses seem to be doing their part to discourage this dangerous habit. Think smoking is cool? grown-up? You won't think so if you don't live long enough to see your own kids graduate from high school.

It's a no-brainer: I WON'T SMOKE. End of story.
(But not the end of me.)

Some individuals—like Walter—accumulate things. Others, like Miss Pomeroy, take a certain pleasure in throwing things out.

—*Walter: The Story of a Rat*
by Barbara Wersba
illustrated by Donna Diamond

Some people can't bear to throw away a broken shoelace. Others don't want anything in the house that isn't new and in use. Neither is right nor wrong. And both can be good, as seen in this story. Walter, a rat who reads and speaks, accumulates a new friend in Miss Pomeroy. And Miss Pomeroy, a writer, discards her preference for solitude in favor of her book-loving housemate, Walter.

Am I an accumulator or a discarder? Or some of each? Whatever, I'll let this be my guiding rule: Keep the good stuff. Especially people. (And critters that read.)

You might think, if you didn't know him well, that he was a stern and serious man. He wasn't. He was actually a wildly funny person.

—*Danny the Champion of the World*
by Roald Dahl
illustrated by Quentin Blake

Would you bite into something without knowing what it is? Swallow something without tasting it? No. You wouldn't eat it until you trusted it. So why are we quicker to judge a person than a vegetable?

Half the problems of the world—heck, maybe three-quarters—are caused by people not getting to know each other well enough. I'm sure I've already made judgments about quite a few people I hardly know. Today I'll pick one and get to know him or her better. My judgment was quick. Now I'll find out how good it was.

W hy did he agree to join? Was it
because he was flattered that
they wanted him?

—"Alien Candy"
Nightmare Hour: Time for Terror
by R. L. Stine

Can you tell the difference between what you want and what your ego wants? It's not always easy, especially when flattery enters the picture. Flattery can dazzle the ego, sweet-talk it into things you may not really want. Be careful. Be honest. Identify yourself and stick to it. When flattery comes purring, give it the cold shoulder and turn back to yourself.

Am I easily flattered? Does flattery weaken me, make me forget who I really am and what I really want? I understand that flattery feels good, and there's nothing wrong with that, but I won't allow it to make me do things I don't really want to do.

"I would like a drink of water, Esther.
I am thirsty."

—*Plain Girl*
by Virginia Sorensen
illustrated by Charles Geer

Call it pop, soda, or a soft drink—it's one of the worst things you can put in your body, especially if you drink it every day. Meanwhile, nature provides the perfect thirst-quencher. It covers three-quarters of the planet, and it comprises over half the human body. You may have heard of it. It's called water.

It's time to wean myself away from liquid sugar, otherwise known as soda. Starting today, I will begin to cut down on my soda consumption. When I'm thirsty, I'll reach for a nice cold glass of water. It may be hard at first, but I'm confident that I can break the liquid sugar habit. And my body will thank me for it.

A boy named Danny Tucker once told her she had a voice like a cricket with a pillow over its head. And she believed him.

—Knitting Nell
by Julie Jersild Roth

Old sayings get to be old because they've proved their worth over time. This one applies here: *Consider the source.* Much of what we think about ourselves—and this is true especially of kids—comes out of the mouths of other people. If something unkind about you comes out of the mouth of an unkind, imperfect person, consider the source.

Everybody gets nailed with unkind words now and then. Why should I be any different? Next time it happens to me, I'll consider the source—and brush those words away like a bug.

To a visitor just passing through, Al-Kal'as appeared to be a prosperous place, but beneath the veneer of prosperity a second city existed— a city of misery.

—*Wishing Moon*
by Michael O. Tunnell

Beware of appearances. It goes for places and it goes for people. That happy-go-lucky kid over there might really be miserable inside.

I'm old enough to understand what great actors people can be—myself included. So even if friends of mine seem happy all the time, I'll make sure they know that I've got a shoulder they can cry on if need be.

"She turned everybody around her
into heroes too."

—*Defining Dulcie*
by Paul Acampora

Among us are a few special people who need no direction, people who set their own pace and lead the way to good things. Maybe you are such a person. If not, one of the best skills you can develop is to identify such people and emulate them. This is copycatting in the best sense.

Today I'll be a copycat. I'll pick out someone I admire,
someone who's doing really good things, and in my own way,
I'll follow.

To be honest, Kate wasn't all that sorry her parents had unplugged the TV.

—*The Secret Language of Girls*
by Frances O'Roark Dowell

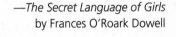

"Unplug the TV?! Oh no—anything but that!!! Ground me till I'm forty but don't take away my TV!!!"

"Are you ready for this? We're unplugging your computer, too."

"AAAARRRRGH!!!"

Is worse torture possible? Is life worth living without your beloved TV? Even for, say, a day? a week? Here's the answer, in tiny letters so it doesn't shock you off your feet:

yes

Beyond the virtual and televised worlds is a real one, with real birdsong and real physical activity and real in-the-flesh organisms known as people.

Am I beginning to confuse the counterfeit world of my glowing screens with the real world? I'll turn off the screens for a day or more—yes, voluntarily, myself!—and find out.

It's amazing what a few kind words and a smile can do for a dog.

—*Hank the Cowdog*
by John R. Erickson
illustrated by Gerald L. Holmes

Or a cat or a goldfish or a hermit crab. Yes, you might get more of a reaction from a dog than a crab, but there's something else to be considered here: In expressing yourself to an animal, whether responsive or not, you are communicating with life; you are adding a little stitch to the fabric that binds all creatures together.

Today I'll say something nice to my pet. If I don't have one, I'll find someone else's. Or go to the pet shop. And next time I see a hermit crab, I'll smile and say "Hi!"

I magine a day . . .
when you don't
need wings
to soar.

—*Imagine a Day*
by Sarah L. Thomson
illustrated by Rob Gonsalves

Some high jumpers play a mental game. They stand before the bar and picture themselves leaping over it again and again. Then they rear back, start their run-up, and jump. If they make it, they believe it's partly because they imagined themselves doing so.

Sometimes life tilts toward imagination. This is good to know, for there's a high bar I'd like to clear. Maybe it has to do with sports or schoolwork or some private personal achievement that only I know about. I'll picture myself clearing the bar until I'm convinced it will happen. Oh . . . and I'll remember that imagination by itself isn't enough— sooner or later, I'll have to jump.

"My," he laughed, "you've got an enviable amount of energy today, don't you?"
"No," I said . . . "I'm just mad."

—*Flipped*
by Wendelin Van Draanen

This kid could become some kind of therapist, because he already understands that there is more than one way to express anger. You don't have to take it out on somebody else—or yourself. Any sort of physical activity will usually do the trick.

Next time I get so mad I feel like hitting somebody, I won't. Instead, I'll dig a hole or run a mile or otherwise energize my tail off till I'm not so mad anymore.

Little lies that make people feel better
are not bad, like thanking someone for
a meal they made even if you hated it,
or telling a sick person they look
better when they don't.

—*Harriet the Spy*
by Louise Fitzhugh

Little lies, white lies, fibs—sure, sometimes they're just the ticket. But it's hard to lay down a general rule: when to little-lie, when not to. Avoiding hurt feelings can't always be your guide. Sometimes truth is better even if it hurts. It's confusing. So for now, let's just say this: If you find that the only one who ever seems to benefit from your lies is you, you'd better revisit this whole subject.

I am old enough now to understand that not every white lie
is bad. But I will resist the temptation to believe that if a
lie comes from me, it must automatically be good.

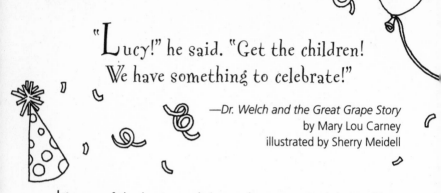

"Lucy!" he said. "Get the children! We have something to celebrate!"

—*Dr. Welch and the Great Grape Story*
by Mary Lou Carney
illustrated by Sherry Meidell

It's one of the best words in our language: *celebrate*. How sad to have a tombstone that reads:

> Many times she was elated
> But she never celebrated

Don't let the happy moments in your life go by without officially recognizing them—maybe with a bite of your favorite candy and a quiet "Thank you" or a loud "Yahoo!" or a party with friends. Doing so will help reinforce your sense that life is good.

It may be big or it may be small, even invisible, but something good will almost certainly happen to me today. When it does, I won't brush it off as if I were entitled to it. I won't be stingy with celebration.

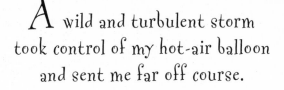

A wild and turbulent storm
took control of my hot-air balloon
and sent me far off course.

—*The Three Golden Keys*
by Peter Sís

This is a metaphor for the unpredictability of life. No matter how hard we try to stick to our plan, something always seems to come along and blow us off course: a bad grade, a rejection, an accident, a new love, a broken heart. Course-changers aren't always bad. Sometimes they point us in an even better direction. Or not. The best you can do is accept the unexpected turbulence into your life, then take it into account as you recompute your plan.

If something blows me off course today, I won't kick and scream and curse my bad luck. I'll accept it as a part of life. And I'll ask: Does this turbulence point me in a new and better direction? Can I/should I turn away from it, or must I learn to live with it? I'll answer these questions, then proceed.

"Do you"—she swallowed—"do you
have any books on learning how
to dance?"

—*Sophie and Lou*
by Petra Mathers

Isn't it great that we live in a world that welcomes questions like Sophie's? Want to learn to dance? Build an airplane? Bake a pie? Shear a sheep? It's hard to think of a learn-to question whose answer cannot be found in a book.

If I want to learn how to do something, I'll begin
at a library or a bookstore.

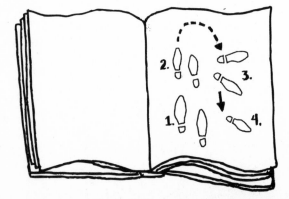

"There are always things to miss," said Maggie. "No matter where you are."

—*Sarah, Plain and Tall*
by Patricia MacLachlan

Maggie is telling us at least two things:

    1. Wherever we are, it's not perfect.

    2. Wherever we are, we should appreciate it and get the most out of it, because once we leave it behind, we're going to miss it.

This town. This home. This school. This day. This moment.
I may be cruising through them with hardly a thought,
but once I move on to another time, another place,
I may wish I were back here and now.
So, today, my motto: *I am this moment.*

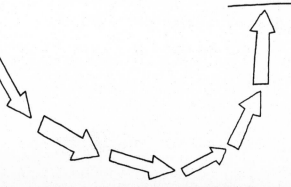

I always tumble into trouble when I lose my temper.

—Robin Hood and His Merry Men
retold by Jane Louise Curry
illustrated by John Lytle

Funny thing about a temper—if it's such a bad thing, shouldn't we *want* to lose it? Let the darn thing go! Good riddance! Not really. Because your temper, you see, is just that—*your* temper—meaning you're stuck with it. If you let it loose, it's only going to circle around like a boomerang and come back and bite you in the butt.

If my temper wants to escape today, I won't let it, because I don't want to be butt-bitten.

Outside the classroom: Martha volunteers at an animal shelter to train dogs so that they have a better chance of being adopted.

—See What You Can Be: Explore Careers That Could Be for You!
by Diane Heiman and Liz Suneby
illustrated by Tracey Wood

Volunteering is a good thing for many reasons. Here are two:

1. When you volunteer, you provide a valuable service for free. In your own little (or not-so-little) way, you make the world a better place. By volunteering, you declare: "I do this because I want to help. Because I care. Not for the money."

2. Volunteering is a terrific—and mucho smart—way to sample various occupations, one of which may lead to your lifetime career.

Volunteering could open up whole new worlds to me.
I'd be foolish not to at least check it out.

Francis Scott Key was a well-known Washington lawyer. . . . On August 31st [1814], he had only just come home, when there was a sharp knock at his door.

—*By the Dawn's Early Light*
by Steven Kroll
illustrated by Dan Andreasen

That knock set in motion events that led to the song we sing at the start of professional games and many other occasions: "The Star-Spangled Banner." The flat facts of history become more real and interesting when we know the stories behind them.

I've seen and heard and stood up for my national anthem all my life, but how much do I really know about it? Today I'll go to the library and find out.

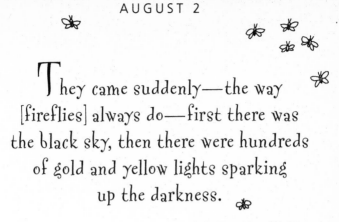

They came suddenly—the way [fireflies] always do—first there was the black sky, then there were hundreds of gold and yellow lights sparking up the darkness.

—*Be Ever Hopeful, Hannalee*
by Patricia Beatty

If you ever get a chance to be a bug, be a firefly. Picture it: nighttime, blackness. You're there, right in front of their noses, but they can't see you. You wait . . . you wait . . . *now!*—turn on your light! "Daddy, look! A lightning bug!"

There are a lot of people out there in the darkness. A lot of smiles waiting to happen.

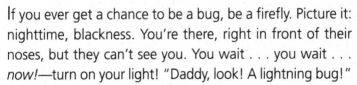

I am a firefly. There is a light within me. Today I will turn it on and brighten a darkness.
I am a firefly.

"Keep your reserves hidden."

—*Shabanu: Daughter of the Wind*
by Suzanne Fisher Staples

Many things could be said about this interesting quote. Let's focus on trust. Let's say you meet someone new and within ten minutes it feels as if you've known each other forever. Before the day is over, you've spilled practically every detail of your life to this new person. Before the week is over, you regret it. Because the new person has spread information that you intended to be private or has otherwise violated your confidence. Leaving you with a lesson learned: Don't give your trust away—let it be earned.

If I meet a new, promising person today, I'll make him or her earn my trust before I reveal my hidden reserves.

"I wanted to write some of my memories in my notebook," said Jack.

—*Stage Fright on a Summer Night*
(Magic Tree House #25)
by Mary Pope Osborne

Memories are like candy wrappers strewn across the pathway of your life: You can follow them back to where you started. Like candy wrappers, memories sometimes blow away with the winds of time. That's why it's a good idea to write them down. It's useful to have memory backup.

Today I'll start a journal. I'll write down what happened today, plus something I remember from another day. I'll do this at least once or twice a week. This will ensure the preservation of my memories. I'll create my own personal history. Someday I'll be glad I did.

The billboard's message still echoed in her head: "LIVE YOUR DREAMS!" Trouble was, Firebird wasn't even sure yet what her dreams were.

—*Beyond the Billboard*
by Susan Gates

But that's OK, Firebird. Of all the definitions of childhood, surely one of them is: a time to find one's dreams. Dreams come from a life lived day by day. You cannot shop for dreams; they will come to you. When that happens—and if you follow the billboard's message—your dreams will give birth to your life.

I have a dream. Has it occurred to me that it doesn't have to remain a dream, a wistful fantasy? Has it occurred to me that I can kick-start my dream? Has it occurred to me that I can make my dream my life? Has it?

And wanting, most of all,
to cheer her up,
[Belle] gave Bea a hug and
filled up her cup.

—*The Friend*
by Sarah Stewart
illustrated by David Small

In the story, Bea has just rescued Belle from drowning. But Belle is thanking her for much more than that. She's thanking her for being there every day of her childhood. You've heard the phrase *fair-weather friend*. That's the person who shows up when things are going great but who never seems to be around when things are not so great. There's not much you can do about fair-weather friends, except to make sure you're not one of them.

Is a friend of mine having a bad time—getting rained on, so to speak? If so, I won't look the other way. I'll bring an umbrella of compassion big enough for both of us.

Feeling the ocean, hearing it, smelling it, but not seeing . . . hurt indescribably.

—*Taking Hold: My Journey into Blindness*
by Sally Hobart Alexander

Author Sally Hobart Alexander cannot see the ocean she is standing in because she is going blind. And at that moment it's not much comfort knowing she can still hear, smell, and feel. The ability to see something ten feet away has become infinitely precious because it is gone.

When someone speaks, do I hear? When I open my eyes in the morning, do they see? If so, whether I believe in God or not, I will look to the sky and say *Thank you!* If not, I will consider how things might be if I had less, and I will say *Thank you!* for what I do have.

Ruby waved, but the woman
didn't wave back.

—*Lumber Camp Library*
by Natalie Kinsey-Warnock
illustrated by James Bernardin

Does your behavior toward others depend on how they respond to you? Are you nice to someone only if you expect niceness in return? Is your motto: If you don't smile back, that's the last smile you'll ever get from me? Sure, it's tempting to adjust our behavior to the responses of others, but don't give up too easily on your own best impulses. Remember, you are responsible only for your own behavior, not others'.

As I go through the day, I'll try to notice whether the behavior of others bends my behavior away from the natural me. If so, I'll make more of an effort to be true to myself.

Charlie: So I should, what—tell myself
I'm better than I am?
Nick: Yeah, exactly. And then you will be.

—"Riding the Pine: A Play"
by Ron Koertge
(from *Baseball Crazy,* edited by Nancy E. Mercado)

What kind of nonsense is this, anyway? you're thinking.
*Even I'm old enough to know that you can't get better just
by saying it to yourself.*

Well, maybe not *just* saying it to yourself—but saying
it to yourself can give you a running start to making it actually happen. Belief, followed by effort, often becomes reality. You will be as good, or not-so-good, as you believe
yourself to be. And belief feeds on words. So—*say it.*

There's something I'd like to be better at, but I have my
doubts. I just don't think it's in me. Today I'll see if I can
begin changing that around. I'll start by telling myself—
out loud in the privacy of my room—what I want to do.
I'll repeat it till I begin to believe. Then I'll start
working to make it come true.

She was determined to become
an expert trick bike rider.

—*Tomboy of the Air: Daredevil Pilot Blanche Stuart Scott*
by Julie Cummins

We don't know how many people told Blanche Stuart Scott "*You* can't become a trick bike rider. You're a girl." And later, at a time when few women drove: "*You* can't drive a car. You're a woman." And still later: "*You* can't do trick flying. You're not a man." In every age there are plenty of people around to remind you what you cannot possibly do. Thank goodness, for these naysayers provide a priceless service: They spur the Blanche Scotts among us to achieve great things.

Is there someone in my life who tells me I can't do this or that? Do I believe such people? Do they discourage me? Do they make me doubt myself? Do they make me want to give up? Or . . . are they nothing more than nature doing me a favor by sending me someone to prove wrong?

Sometimes I think you have to
live through something yourself before
you can really understand it.

—*Fast Sam, Cool Clyde, and Stuff*
by Walter Dean Myers

Do you agree with that? If so, then you understand why adults are always saying stuff like "You'll see. Just wait till you grow up" and "Someday you'll understand." In the meantime, cut those know-it-all grown-ups some slack and just wait for that "someday" to arrive.

Even though sometimes I think I've got it all figured out,
I know I really don't. If today is like most other days,
something is bound to happen that I don't understand.
Maybe the answer lies a few years down the road.
That's cool. I can wait.

Garden patch
Rake and hoe
Carrots sprouting in a row . . .

—*At Grandma's*
by Rhonda Gowler Greene
illustrated by Karla Firehammer

Did you ever pull a carrot from the earth? Or do you believe that carrots come from the produce aisle in the supermarket? Do you believe that string beans come from string bean machines and turnips from turnip molds? Have you ever set foot on a farm or in a vegetable garden? Ever?

Two hundred years ago my country was mostly farms. Now it's mostly houses, parking lots, and drugstores, or so it seems. I have lost contact with the earth that feeds me. Today I will track down a vegetable in its native habitat and in this small way reconnect with my human roots.

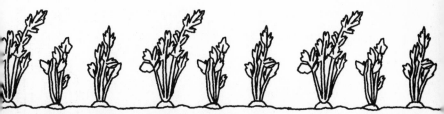

"None of us can do all the things that will save the planet but each of us can do some of them and all of that will add up and be better than nothing."

—*Earth to Matthew*
by Paula Danziger

Spill something on the floor at school, and what happens? A custodian comes along and cleans it up. Mess up the earth, and what happens? Nothing—unless *you* do something. For you are—each of us is—the custodian of our ultimate Home.

Today I may or may not clean up my room—but I *will* go outside and clean up my Home.

I know you can ask the ocean for shells.

—*Out of the Ocean*
by Debra Frasier

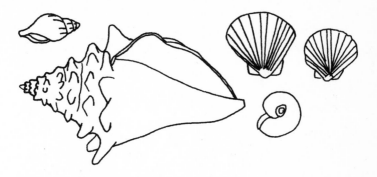

And the mountain for white birches . . . and the sky for clouds . . . and the land for grass. It's a giving place we earthlings live in, this third planet from the sun. And if truth be told, we don't even have to ask—although, come to think of it, "please" and "thank you" would be nice.

Today I will kneel down by a flower or tree, and I will whisper "Thank you."

"Doesn't anything interest you?"

—*Strange Happenings*
by Avi

Some kids think it's uncool to show interest. Their slouchy attitude yawns "Whatever." Too bad. Those kids are missing a fascinating world in which, as the poet Walt Whitman wrote, the lowly mouse is a "miracle." You as a human being are programmed to respond to the wonders around you. Don't fight it.

I won't fight it. If that means being uncool, tough tomatoes. I'm interested in lots of stuff, and I don't mind showing it.

Mr. Penderwick believed in long walks.
One of his favorite sayings was,
Take a walk, clear your head.

—*The Penderwicks: A Summer Tale of Four Sisters,
Two Rabbits, and a Very Interesting Boy*
by Jeanne Birdsall

When was the last time you did that—took a walk? Not to go to a particular place but just for the sake of the walk itself? Try it, and make this interesting discovery: One end of your body (head) can benefit from action on the other end (feet).

My head is cluttered. Junked up. Bursting at the seams. It could use a good airing out. I'll do my poor overstuffed head a favor: I'll take a walk.

She came home at dusk,
tired and dusty,
smelling of sweat and horses.

—"Yes, It Was My Grandmother"
by Luci Tapahonso
(from *More Spice Than Sugar: Poems About Feisty Females*,
compiled by Lillian Morrison, illustrated by Ann Boyajian)

Not long ago, girls were not supposed to sweat. It was considered unladylike. Even today, if a little girl-kid likes to rough it up and get dirty and would rather climb a tree than burp a doll, she's called a "tomboy," as if she were not 100% girl. Sure, we've made progress. It's OK for girls to sweat. Now let's give them all the freedom they need to be fully themselves.

Declaration: I hereby excuse all girls from conforming to the 19th century standard of "ladylike." If a girl wants to be ladylike, that's fine. If not, that's just as fine.

Soon our money
was
all
gone.

—*The Adventures of the Dish and the Spoon*
by Mini Grey

The most frightening of the six words above is *soon*. It's amazing how fast money disappears. It's kind of like summer vacation. Looking ahead, it seems as if it will never end; looking back, you wonder where it all went.

I've learned (I hope) not to waste my summer vacation time,
because I understand that it doesn't last forever.
Now I'll take what I've learned about summer vacation
and apply it to my money.

W hen you're exploring, the best
thing is that you don't know what's
coming next. That's the most
frightening thing, too.

—*That Wild Berries Should Grow*
by Gloria Whelan

Both "best" and "frightening"? Does that make sense? When it comes to exploring the unknown—yes. Volunteering to visit a retirement home, joining a club, speaking to an interesting-looking student—venturing into the unknown can indeed be frightening. And the discoveries you make can be the best.

Am I content to sit back in the rocking chair of my life?
Or am I brave enough to explore the unknown territory of
my future, my abilities, my opportunities? Today I'll take at
least one step into some unexplored territory of my life.

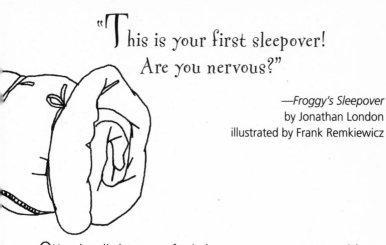

"This is your first sleepover!
Are you nervous?"

—*Froggy's Sleepover*
by Jonathan London
illustrated by Frank Remkiewicz

OK, what little gem of wisdom can we come up with regarding sleepovers? That they hark back to primitive tribespeople and their instinct to huddle with others against the dreadful night? That in sleeping over we bond in mysterious ways? Maybe so, but let's leave all that deep stuff for another book. For us, here's all that needs to be said as you head off to your first—or your tenth—sleepover: Have fun!

*Have I been reluctant to join a sleepover—at my friends',
my school, my grandparents'? Maybe I'm forgetting
that the whole point is simply to have fun.
Maybe I should reconsider.*

Every painting is a magic window
that your own imagination can open
wide and climb through.

—*A Quiet Place*
by Douglas Wood
illustrated by Dan Andreasen

Alice stepped through a looking glass, so why can't you climb into a painting? Look at a painting with only your eyes, and it remains nothing more than a flat picture on a flat wall. But look at it with your imagination—ah, then you can almost hear it say "Please come in."

Today I will look for a picture that appeals to me.
When I find one, I'll climb in.

AUGUST 22

Go outside
and face the east
and greet the sun
with some kind of blessing

—*The Way to Start a Day*
by Byrd Baylor
illustrated by Peter Parnall

Salute the sun as a soldier salutes the flag each morning. You are blessed with another day—another day to color with a kind word, a good deed, a friendly touch. Another day to experience this miracle you've been granted—this *life*. Celebrate!

Today I promise this: Someday I will awaken early enough to go outside and face the east and greet the rising sun.

A ccidents happen when you
get frustrated or when you're in
too much of a hurry.

—*Cooking Wizardry for Kids*
by Margaret Kenda and Phyllis S. Williams

After a minute of pushing and pulling, your dresser drawer is still stuck open, allowing the world to see your underwear. So you swing your leg back and give it one good kick. . . .

You have five minutes to eat and be out of the house. Nobody's picking up the ringing phone. Something catches your eye out the kitchen window, so you look up from the tomato you're slicing with a very sharp knife. . . .

Sometimes accidents can't be helped; sometimes they can.
Today I'll begin practicing haste- and frustration-control.
Someday, when I'm driving a car, this may save a life.

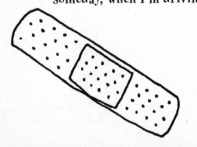

There was peace and harmony in the kingdom once again, except for the little troubles that came up every so often even in the best of circumstances, since nothing is perfect.

—*The Real Thief*
by William Steig

Peace and harmony do not require perfection. Thank goodness for that—because life so often seems to be an itch here, a glitch there, a mess waiting to happen. Harmony is flexible. It bends with imperfection. So should you.

I declare today Dry Armpit Day.
I will not sweat the small stuff.

*C*ats are patient. Even when they are anxious and frightened, they will wait quietly, watching to see what happens.

—*Catwings Return*
by Ursula K. Le Guin
illustrated by S. D. Schindler

Cats float on time. They seem to know that, just by their being still, time's current will carry them from happen to happen, from moment to better moment to best moment. Sometimes we would do well to copy a cat.

Today I won't let impatience get the best of me. I'll give things a chance to unfold. I'll wait for time to carry me to the next—and maybe better—moment.

Good-bye is always hello to something else.

—*Borrowed Children*
by George Ella Lyon

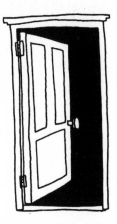

Arrival is the flip side of departure. Goodbye, Monday; hello, Tuesday. Goodbye, Malcolm; hello, Sam. How do you want to walk your life? Backward, facing Goodbye? Or forward, facing Hello?

What have I said goodbye to lately? (Or what has said goodbye to me?) Am I walking my life backward, still saying "Goodbye" to yesterday? If so, I'll turn around and see who or what is waiting to greet me today.

"We have no choice of what color we're born or who our parents are or whether we're rich or poor. What we do have is some choice over what we make of our lives once we're here."

—*Roll of Thunder, Hear My Cry*
by Mildred D. Taylor

Your life belongs to you. And unless you believe you'll come back in another life as a king or a turtle or whatever, this is the only life you'll ever have—here on earth, anyway. Therefore, how do you account for perhaps the most spectacularly incredible thing we can say about the human race: Many of us waste and fritter away our one and only life!

Today I will recognize my life as the precious, irreplaceable gift that it is. Although I sometimes think my life will last forever, I understand that it will not. Therefore, I will choose not to waste it.

It would be terrible to wake up and not know your name, not know who you were.

—*The Bumblebee Flies Anyway*
by Robert Cormier

The universe comes in two parts: (1) you and (2) everything else. Only when the two come together, fit well together, is the world—*your* world—complete. (Kind of like this book isn't really "complete" until you pick it up and read it.) Another way of saying this: If you don't make sense to yourself, nothing else will. Now, here's the really cool part. Every night when you go to sleep, the universe separates into its two parts. Like an engine from a passenger train, you decouple from everything else and go floating off to a restorative void without names, time, or space. And then it's morning, and for the first groggy moment, you have no idea who you are, and then, there on the pillow with you, is your identity, your self—and the world falls back into place.

I have a new appreciation of the sleep/wake cycle, and I look forward to tomorrow morning and the daily miracle of rejoining myself and completing the universe.

Seems people knew she saw
the very best of them.

—*Missing May*
by Cynthia Rylant

Does it bother you that people may not give you enough credit, may not see the best in you? Consider this: Maybe one of the best things about you is your habit of seeing the best in others. If it's not, maybe it should be. And if so, does it show?

Not to brag, but I know I have some good points, some reasons to feel good about myself. And, sure, sometimes I wish they were more obvious to others. I mean, what am I supposed to do, wear a big sign saying HEY, LOOK AT ME— I'M WONDERFUL? On the other hand, am I as sharp as I should be at seeing the good points in others? Today's reminder: It works both ways.

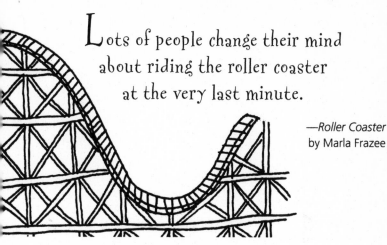

Lots of people change their mind
about riding the roller coaster
at the very last minute.

—*Roller Coaster*
by Marla Frazee

You've probably found this out already: Life is one big, fat roller-coaster ride after another. Boyfriends, girlfriends, friend friends, school, family—everything is a loopy ride, and sometimes you just can't know if you want to hop aboard until the coaster rolls into your station and the door swings open. And suddenly it's real, it's close, it's *now*. And now is the time to remember this: Just because you have a ticket in your hand doesn't mean you have to use it. If you don't like the way you feel, if you don't like the looks of this ride up close, then toss your ticket in the trash can and walk away.

**If I'm asked to do something today that deep down
I don't really want to do, I won't.**

*H*e had lost a risky bet.

—*Tops and Bottoms*
by Janet Stevens

It's one thing to lay down a small bet now and then—but beware! Gambling can be habit-forming, like drugs and smoking and alcohol. People begin gambling for two reasons: (1) to make quick and easy money and (2) excitement. Both reasons collapse before this simple fact: Most betters lose. Gambling, you see, is merely a quick and easy and exciting way to throw away your money.

OK, now and then, when I'm old enough, I may buy myself a lottery ticket. But I'm not going to gamble away my hard-earned money. As for excitement, I'll get all I need from games themselves, not from betting on them.

"A true outdoorsman is prepared for everything!" said Maxwell to his mother.

—*Maxwell's Mountain*
by Shari Becker
illustrated by Nicole Wong

And so what does Maxwell do as he prepares to climb the mountain? He puts some cookies in his pocket. He doesn't just go charging off blindly up the mountain. He tries to think ahead. In effect, he fast-forwards the movie of his life until he sees himself on the mountain and can figure out what he might need when he actually gets there. Maxwell is only a kid, but in some ways he's a pretty good role model to follow.

Am I a plunger and a charger? Do I dive into things and places without a thought to what I might need when I get there? I've got a head on my shoulders. I'll use it to be prepared, with cookies or whatever.

Learning is not the accumulation of knowledge, but rather, one thing only: understanding.

—*Bound*
by Donna Jo Napoli

If you don't know this already, you will in years to come. When you look back on your school days and remember your teachers, the ones you will remember most fondly are those who not only made you memorize dates and gave you tests but also led you to the threshold of understanding, who helped you to see *why* a particular date is important and *how* a particular fact fits into your life.

Sometimes it seems as if school does nothing but torment me with tests and bog me down with useless dates and facts. Is it possible that my teachers are also opening doors of understanding for me? Is it possible that I can begin to figure out this world I was born into if only I will step through those doorways? If a teacher opens a door for me today, I will enter.

Snail-mail once a month.

—Sloppy Firsts
by Megan McCafferty

Even if it's just a postcard. Don't let good old letter-writing die out completely.

OK, I'll follow the direction above—I'll snail-mail somebody, no matter how short the message, at least once a month.

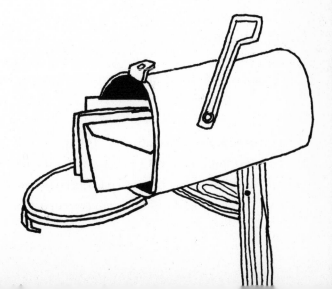

Though mountain gorillas probably never existed in huge numbers, today only six hundred remain in the world.

—*Gorilla Walk*
by Ted and Betsy Lewin

Six hundred. Not enough to fill a school auditorium. Six hundred. One of the most magnificent creatures ever to walk the earth. Six hundred heartbeats away from extinction. Six billion of us. Six hundred of them.

The Number of the Day: 600. The Irreplaceable Treasure of the Day: mountain gorillas. Will tomorrow's number be 599? Today I'll Google *mountain gorilla* and save and see if I can help stop it from happening.

W hen Lucy's house got too loud,
she went to the library.

—*Lucy's Quiet Book*
by Angela Shelf Medearis
illustrated by Lisa Campbell Ernst

Isn't it nice to know there's a place like the library? For those times when you want mild, not wild. A place that's always the same, that welcomes you, that says "Come on in, friend—out of the cold, out of the heat, out of the noise." Think of the library as your *other* room.

Today I'll make myself at home in the library.

"We'll do what we can, you and I.
After that's done, we'll figure
what to do next."

—*The Wheel on the School*
by Meindert DeJong
illustrated by Maurice Sendak

Kids are often criticized for acting thoughtlessly and impulsively. Yet some situations demand fast action more than long-term planning: You come upon an accident, you find yourself or others in danger, someone needs help *now*. Sometimes your brain should take a backseat to your best instincts. Sometimes, especially in emergencies, the rule is: Do now, think later.

I act without thinking sometimes. (OK, more than sometimes.) And today I'll try to start changing that. But I won't totally eliminate it. I'll stay flexible enough so that if I find myself in a situation demanding fast action, I'll let my best instincts take over.

"Welcome to the world.
It's a great place to be."

—*Hedgehog's Secret*
by Lena Anderson

OK, sure, there are plenty of days when the world isn't so great—but, hey, it's the only world we've got, right? And don't a lot of those nongreat days say more about us than about the world? Imagine yourself cramped in darkness for nine months, hearing the chatter and laughter and music on the other side of your mother's belly button—who wouldn't itch to be born?

Just because today stinks doesn't mean I have to
blame it on the world. Maybe if I manage my own
personal world a little better, the wider world
will start coming up great.

I don't like being short.

—*How to Make Friends with a Giant*
by Gennifer Choldenko
illustrated by Amy Walrod

Short. Tall. Fair. Dark. Blue eyes. Brown eyes. Freckles. Freckleless. Graceful. Clumsy. We're not clones. We're different. Until someone figures out how to stretch or shrink the human body, we're pretty much stuck with our height and a lot of other dimensions. That's why one of life's keys is to create our happiness from what we *do* have, not from what we don't have. How sad to see a life summed up thus:

HERE LIES JOHN DOE
HE WANTED TO BE SOMEBODY ELSE

Except for a couple of kids who seem to think they're perfect, I'm like most everybody else: There are a few things about myself I'd like to change. Well, if I can change them, fine. If I can't, that's OK, too. I'm not going to waste my life mooning over somebody I'm not.

"Why this unattractive place?"
"It's not unattractive to the pig."

—*On the Far Side of the Mountain*
by Jean Craighead George

This exchange takes place during a search for a girl and her pig, but it has widespread application. It touches on the fact that ours are not the only eyes that see, ours not the only opinion that counts. It's an idea that reaches from daily interaction with classmates and friends to the very pillars of democracy.

There's nothing wrong with having an opinion. Heck, I've got plenty of them. And there's nothing wrong with standing up for my opinions. But there is something wrong with denying others the right to have opinions that differ from mine.

In addition to having us act out the books, the older brothers and sisters used to read to us little kids.

—*The Neddiad*
by Daniel Pinkwater

We should all be so lucky, to have such terrific older siblings. Not every teacher stands at the head of a classroom. Family, friends, experience—all enroll us as students. And none compels our attention more than an older brother or sister.

Everyone is—or should be—a teacher. If I have younger siblings, I'll make sure they wind up with memories like those of the kids in *The Neddiad*. And if there are no little kids in my house, well, there are other houses around.

The violence of major news events
made him feel helpless.

—*Bambert's Book of Missing Stories*
by Reinhardt Jung

The violence of news events makes everyone feel helpless. Having to confront this unfortunate reality is a downside, you might say, of growing up. But let's make this distinction: While it may be true that you *feel* helpless, that doesn't mean you *are* helpless. Setting a tone of nonviolence in your own life, establishing yourself as a peaceful person, can definitely help influence major news events when multiplied by millions of other peaceful people.

I'm still not sure how I feel about all the adult-world issues I'm growing into, but here's one thing I know already: I hate violence. I hate it and I'm not afraid to say so. I will strive to lead a peaceful life and to set an example for others. It's the least I can do. I am *not* helpless.

A worry can feel like a heavy sack
is on your back.

—*Is a Worry Worrying You?*
by Ferida Wolff and Harriet May Savitz
illustrated by Marie Le Tourneau

If you had a heavy sack on your back, what would you do? Drop it right then and there? Haul it to wherever it belongs and drop it there? Ask someone to help you carry it? Dump it in a truck bed? Pay someone to take it off your hands? You might choose any of these options or some other. For sure, there's only one you would never choose: Carry it forever.

Have I been lugging a heavy sack of worry around?
No more. There are plenty of ways to unload it, and that's
what I'm going to do. Forever ends today.

At that time I loved doing things for older people. I liked running to do someone a favor, to get some sugar or tea, or to carry a message.

—*Facing the Lion: Growing Up Maasai on the African Savanna*
by Joseph Lemasolai Lekuton

Why do you think Joseph loved doing things for older people? Maybe because they were thankful. They showed him their gratitude. And in so doing gave back to him more than he gave to them.

Unlike so many kids—and I have to admit I'm one of them—older people do not take little, ordinary, everyday kindnesses for granted. They show their appreciation. It's a feel-good payoff that I want to experience for myself. Today I will.

Everything we do today means that we, and our families, are going to be living with the consequences tomorrow.

—*The Down-to-Earth Guide to Global Warming*
by Laurie David and Cambria Gordon

Global warming is not a figment of some scientist's imagination. It's real, it's already here, and it's threatening just about every living thing on earth—including us. What can we—what can *you*—do about it?

For starters, I can ask my parents and teachers about global warming. I can read a book about it. I can find out what I can do to help right here in my own home and school. That's what I can do. For butterflies and frogs and polar bears and coral reefs. For me. Starting today.

"Did you apologize?"
"Sort of, but he wouldn't let me
talk to him."
"Well, give him some time,
then try again."

—*The Watsons Go to Birmingham—1963*
by Christopher Paul Curtis

Apology is a vital form of communication, of relationship maintenance. *I'm sorry* are two of the most powerful words in our language, especially when they are not flipped blithely over the shoulder but spoken from the heart. They help restore order, balance, harmony. They reduce pain. They heal broken friendship. If they were medicine, they'd be called a miracle.

From now on I'll be sensitive enough to know when I owe an apology and mature enough to say it—and mean it.

I remembered what Clayton had said. People always say words can't hurt you, but that isn't true. They can hurt worse than a punch in the eye.

—*Mayfield Crossing*
by Vaunda Micheaux Nelson

It serves a purpose, telling little kids not to sweat name-calling—"sticks and stones . . ." and all that. But you're old enough now to know it's not that simple. Words can absolutely hurt, hurt deeply. With this big-kid knowledge comes a responsibility: Be careful what you say.

I have it in my power to hurt someone with nothing more than a word. Maybe sticks and stones can break a bone, but words can break a heart. I'll be careful what I say.

He measured the number of lentils
it would take to dam up the Nile and
studied whether porcupines liked
sweet potatoes or yams.

—*The Squishiness of Things*
by Marc Kompaneyets

Put a little fun in your education. Take a break from the usual equations and problems and research topics. Put your learning skills to use in ways not covered in the classroom.

For example: Take any grouping of seven letters in the alphabet (a through *g*, *p* through *v*, etc.) and see how many words you can make from them. Or, using a tape measure and an orange or a grapefruit, determine the volume of the fruit.

I've been solving *their* problems since first grade.
Today I'll make up a problem of *my* own and solve it—
and have fun doing it.

I sat there looking at it,
proud of my work.

—*A House of Tailors*
by Patricia Reilly Giff

That feeling of pride can come from the littlest, most ordinary things. Sweeping a floor. Sewing a button. Carving a jack-o'-lantern. Don't just do it and walk away. Step back. Take a look. Admire. You did well. Enjoy the feeling.

Next time I finish a task or make something, I'll reward myself with a moment to feel good about it. Why cheat myself out of such a simple pleasure?

Writing to Peter Collinson in London to thank him for the gift, Franklin said . . .

—*A Dangerous Engine: Benjamin Franklin,*
from Scientist to Diplomat
by Joan Dash
illustrated by Dušan Petričić

Maybe you're thinking: A curious quote to include in this book. Admittedly, it is an unquote-like quote, but it models a simple transaction in which whatever Franklin said is beside the point. The point is, it portrays the passing of gratitude from one person to another, a practice that is no less than a cornerstone of civilized behavior. And a courtesy too often ignored, too often underdone.

Today I will thank someone for a gift given to me. The gift may not have come in wrapping paper and ribbons. It may have been a favor, a gesture, a word. I may say my gratitude or I may write it, but I won't underdo it. It won't be a tossed-off "Thanx." It will be an old-fashioned, fully felt "Thank you."

"If enough people think of a thing and work hard enough at it, I guess it's pretty nearly bound to happen."

—*By the Shores of Silver Lake*
by Laura Ingalls Wilder
illustrated by Garth Williams

Wonderful stories are told of people who do great things all by themselves. But sometimes it takes a bunch. Sometimes the best way—the only way—to get a good thing done is to join a crowd.

Is there a group of people trying to accomplish something in my school? in my community? on my planet? Do I believe it's a good thing they're trying to do? If so, I'll join up with them today.

In order to finish before the cold weather returned, they gave up their much-loved visits to the countryside.

—*Angelo*
by David Macaulay

Do you remember the first time you were faced with this choice: Do I (1) go play or (2) finish my chore or homework? If you went with (2), that was the day you began to grow up. That was the day the little kid in you accepted the fact that sometimes "I want to" must give way to "I should."

I'm a big kid now. I know the difference between "want to" and "should." I won't let this day go by without finishing whatever it is that I should do.

They had reached their goal.

—*Two Bad Ants*
by Chris Van Allsburg

And now what? This book you're reading says now it's time to simply enjoy what you've accomplished. The race is won. Step off the hot, hard track onto the infield. Take off your spiked shoes. Feel the cool grass underfoot. Relax. The next race will begin soon enough.

What's the point of working my tail off to achieve something if I don't even take time to enjoy it? I'll make sure my life is a healthy balance of work and play.

But the journey Ray Charles took
to stardom was long and hard.

—*Ray Charles*
by Sharon Bell Mathis
illustrated by George Ford

You may not be seeking stardom, but you would like to achieve some sort of success, right? Maybe it's driving your dream car. Or being able to afford season tickets to your favorite team. Or becoming a vet. So when you picture yourself reaching your goal, how long do you imagine it takes? A day or two? A week? A month? Reality check: Overnight success almost never happens. It often takes years. But that's OK. Because, as most successful people will tell you, getting there is half the fun.

When I think about what I want to achieve, am I realistic
or living in a dreamworld? In terms of becoming successful,
I make these two pledges:
1. I will not be scared away by how long it may take.
2. I will have fun along the way.

"[A s your teacher] I work for you."

—*Borrowed Children*
by George Ella Lyon

I work for you. Not for myself. Not for my pension. For *you*. And not just in the classroom. To make you a better student. A better person. To show you the way to a fulfilling life.

Today I will thank a teacher for working for me. If I'm too shy to say it out loud, I'll write a note. If I'm too shy to sign my name, I'll sign "A Grateful Student."

She was tired of being a copycat anyway.

—*The Costume Copycat*
by Maryann Macdonald
illustrated by Anne Wilsdorf

Sometimes it's fine to copy someone—a style, a good habit, etc. It's one of the ways we learn. And maybe it's flattering to the person being copied. But sooner or later you'll want to strike out on your own, establish your own identity, reap the rewards of being yourself.

I'm not too proud to imitate and learn from the best in someone else. But I will use imitation only to get started. Then I will cease being a copy of that someone else and become my own cat.

Got Geography!

—*Got Geography!*
Poems selected by Lee Bennett Hopkins
illustrated by Philip Stanton

Today we're not looking at a quote from a book but rather the title of the book itself, because this title, complete with exclamation point, says it all. Can you imagine attending a school for three years and not knowing the way to the gym? Or living in a town for three years and not knowing your way around? Well, there are a lot of kids who have lived in this country all their lives and they still don't know North Dakota from North Carolina.

It's my country, my planet. Today I'll get a map of the USA. I'll start by acquainting myself with the locations of the fifty states. I'll start with North Dakota.

"But sometimes you do take too much on yourself."

—*M. C. Higgins, the Great*
by Virginia Hamilton

Does your eye twitch? Does your stomach rumble? Are you awake when you should be sleeping? Sleepy when you should be alert? As you go to bed at night, does it strike you that you haven't taken a deep breath all day? *Yes* answers may mean you're overloaded. Be warned: Overloaded electrical circuits snap out, and so do overloaded people. It's better to do five things well than ten things half-well.

Do I tend to bite off more than I can chew? Sure, I want to be active and productive, but not at the expense of my health. Because if I snap out, I'll be doing nothing well.

The new kid at school seems so shy,
He can barely mumble out "Hi!"

—*There Once Was a Very Odd School*
by Stephen Krensky
illustrated by Tamara Petrosino

Everybody is the "new kid" at one time or another. It's not that you're not friendly—you're just new, you're shy. All you really want is for somebody to come up to you and say "Hi." Remember that next time *you* run into a new kid.

Today I'll keep a lookout for a new kid.
If I find one, I'll say "Hi."

"Wheeeeeee!"

—*The Three Pigs*
by David Wiesner

The sound quoted above is that of someone breaking free—in this case, three pigs who have just escaped from the big, bad wolf and the story they were trapped in. When they realize it is not a story of their own making or choosing, they find a way out.

Are you living a story written by someone else? Are you the author of your own life? Or does your life have a hundred other authors, telling you what to say, what to wear, what to believe, what to think?

My words, my thoughts, my actions—do they really come from me? Or am I following a script written by my peers? Every time I express an opinion or a judgment today, I'll stop and ask myself if it really comes from me. I want to live my own story, not someone else's.

"It's my happy wagon. . . . When something makes me happy, I put a pebble in the wagon. If I'm unhappy, I take a pebble out."

—*Stargirl*
by Jerry Spinelli

Keeping score of happiness may not be for everybody, but it works for Stargirl. And for the tiny Himalayan nation of Bhutan, which calculates and monitors its Gross National Happiness. With many desirable rights to choose from, our Founding Fathers cited only three to justify their declaration of independence: life, liberty, and the pursuit of happiness. Yet we don't so much pursue happiness as let it randomly splash onto us. Tracking happiness helps remind us that this inalienable right doesn't pursue us; we must pursue it.

Come to think of it, when it comes to happiness, I guess I sort of wait around for it to catch me. Chances are I could be happier, but it's all pretty fuzzy because I don't even keep score. And, anyway, how am I supposed to go about *pursuing* happiness? Hel-loo? . . . Maybe following the suggestions in this book would be a good start.

"Don't forget, people," he said as the last bell rang. "Your projects are due next Friday."

—*Semiprecious*
by D. Anne Love

How many of those students do you think will wait until next Thursday to get started? Whether it's a project, a chore, a payment, or an apology, we just love to put things off. Then hate ourselves for being too late. When will we ever learn?

I'm going to try something new. I'm going to *not* wait till the last minute to begin my next project. I'm going to experience a grand new world: the World of Those Who Finish with Plenty of Time to Spare.

"I can't go to a square dance!
You have to dance with everybody
at a square dance!"

—*Temporary Times, Temporary Places*
by Barbara Robinson

Which is maybe *exactly* why every school should have a
square dance.

*Square dance?! Are you kidding? Can you imagine the Goths
dancing with the preppies? The brainiacs with the video
bangers? The twirl girls with the chess players? The world
would never be the same again. Square dance?! That might
lead to—oh no!—talking to each other . . . getting to know
each other . . . maybe even . . . even . . . liking each other!
Hmmm . . . square dance, huh? . . .*

"[My dad] loves to ask questions
that you should never answer.
All adults do this."

—*My Life as a Fifth-Grade Comedian*
by Elizabeth Levy

Sometimes they're trick questions just to tease you; sometimes they may be serious. Questions such as: "Whose
pancakes do you like better—mine or Mom's?" Such as:
"When I'm old, will you rub my feet every day?" Such as:
"Who will you name your first baby after?" Questions that
require you to choose among loved ones or to commit to
a far future you can barely imagine—answer them at your
peril. Or plead the Kids' Fifth Amendment—the Right to
Keep Your Mouth Shut—on the grounds that an answer
may tend to get you into trouble.

If I get a tricky question today, a question that makes me
uncomfortable or that seems unfair, I'll smile and plead the
Kids' Fifth and say "No comment."

There are no radios, stereos or tape players and no posters of rock stars decorate their bedroom.

—*Growing Up Amish*
by Richard Ammon

And when they go someplace, it's in a horse-drawn buggy, not a car. The Amish, they can't be for real, can they? Maybe it's all showbiz. Maybe at the end of the day, when all the picture-taking tourists go away, the Amish pull off their fake beards and climb into their cars and head off to the nearest mall, like everybody else.

Or maybe not. I'll look into it, find out if the Amish are for real. If so, I'll read up on them. Maybe rent the DVD of *Witness*. Not that I'm going to start dreaming about my first buggy instead of my first car! But the fact is they're here, the Amish, and they seem pretty happy, even though they look so unlike me and live so differently from me. I wonder if they know something I don't. I wonder if there's something I can learn from them.

"Do not ever be afraid to start over."

—*Esperanza Rising*
by Pam Muñoz Ryan

GAME OVER

The most interesting word in the quote above is *afraid*. Think about it. Why should the simple act of starting over be something to be afraid of? Is it because starting over is an admission that we've failed to succeed the first time around? Does starting over force us to face the fact that— *gulp!*—we're imperfect?

Sometime today, or tomorrow, I'm going to screw up.
I'll do something poorly or at least not as well as I could.
When that happens, I won't be afraid to try again.
Because I know that starting over is no disgrace.
Failure, you don't scare me.

"Do your work with a good will."

—*Black Beauty*
by Anna Sewell

Poor *work*. Was there ever a word with a bigger bum rap? Do you think of *work* as the opposite of *play*? the opposite of *fun*? If so, get ready for a shocker. Throw yourself into your *work* with the same gusto that you *play* with—and don't be surprised if you find yourself having *fun*.

Today I'll try to think of home*work* as home*play*.

"It's for the best."

—*Keeping the Moon*
by Sarah Dessen

Parents are always saying stuff like this, right? As if they can predict the future. How do they know that *their* way is best? How do they know that *your* way isn't best? What are you supposed to do—just take their word for it?

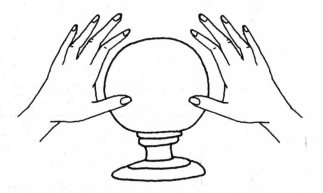

Well, uh, actually, yeah . . . just for the heck of it. Just to throw them a curve. Next time they act like the Great Predictors of My Future, I'll shock the eyebrows off them—I'll take their word for it.

"I know you think the world revolves around you, but it doesn't."

—*The Day My Mother Left*
by James Prosek

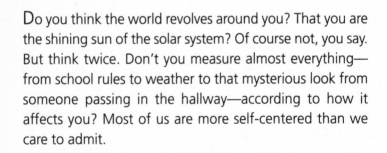

Do you think the world revolves around you? That you are the shining sun of the solar system? Of course not, you say. But think twice. Don't you measure almost everything—from school rules to weather to that mysterious look from someone passing in the hallway—according to how it affects you? Most of us are more self-centered than we care to admit.

Today I will set aside a half hour to extinguish my ego and experience the world without myself at the center.

With the nearest neighbors about a mile away, Alec and his brothers and sisters learned to amuse themselves.

—*With a Little Luck: Surprising Stories of Amazing Discoveries*
by Dennis Brindell Fradin

It seems to be a lost art these days—amusing ourselves, especially if there's no computer screen handy. Would you believe that kids in the "old days" had a great time making fans out of Popsicle sticks? And spinning yo-yos? And reading?

If I find myself alone today with the dreaded Nothing to Do, I'll experiment. I won't turn on the TV or computer or phone a friend. Instead, I'll find my own creative way to banish boredom. Maybe I'll even become a pioneer—the first person in history to replace Nothing to Do with a brand-new-never-been-done-before Something to Do.

"White is something just like black is something. Everybody born on this earth is something and nobody, no matter what color, is better than anybody else."

—*Roll of Thunder, Hear My Cry*
by Mildred D. Taylor

Do you think you're better than some other kid in school? Just because of your color? your address? your grades? Don't be too quick to answer "No!" Prejudice can be sneaky. It can infect us without our knowing it.

Today I will run a prejudice check on myself. If I find some, I'll come back to this page and reread the quote above.

If you've been up all night and cried till you have no more tears left in you—you will know that there comes in the end a sort of quietness.

—*The Lion, the Witch and the Wardrobe*
by C. S. Lewis

When we are out of balance, it is in our nature to shed water: sweat, urine, tears. Tears don't make our unhappiness disappear, but they do muffle its clamor, blunt its edge, give us a bit of relief, help us get ready to cope with tomorrow.

If one of life's hard times hits me today, I'll remember that a good cry might help.

"We can only do the best we can
with what we have."

—*The Door in the Wall*
by Marguerite de Angeli

A cowboy in a TV series said, "There's nothing sadder than a donkey trying to be a racehorse." The people-point here is that we're all different. We are who we are. The secret lies not in trying to be somebody else but in discovering who we ourselves are and making the best of it.

What territory, what potential, lies within me that I have not yet explored? Why am I wasting my time imitating other kids when there's plenty of *me* waiting to be discovered? Will the real me please stand up?

"Losing's just a number on a scoreboard."

—*Onion John*
by Joseph Krumgold

There! Now don't you feel silly? Look at all the time you've wasted thinking that losing is a big deal, thinking that if you lost, you must be a loser. What a dummy! How could you not know that the only "loser" in this world is one number per scoreboard? And even that doesn't last long. Because what happens to all those numbers at the ends of all those games—winners and losers alike? *They all go back to zero!*

Sure, I might come up short on a scoreboard today, but I'll leave that number behind and go home a winner by my own definition. I decline to be defined by a number.

"She kept a fiery eye out to make sure
no one removed any books
from the shelves."

—*The Library Dragon*
by Carmen Agra Deedy
illustrated by Michael P. White

Let's hope your library is not guarded by a dragon but rather by a helpful human, ready, anxious even, to be your guide through a wonderland of adventure and knowledge.

Do I make good use of my library? Or do I act as if it were being guarded by a dragon? Today I'm going to stop by my library—school or public—and take out a book and say hello, and thank you, to the librarian.

Every step Pal took
seemed to rattle my bones.

—*Mrs. Mack*
by Patricia Polacco

Pal is a horse. Pat's first horse. Riding Pal is not a pleasant experience for Pat. It hurts. But she sticks with it because the joy and satisfaction of becoming a rider outweigh the butt-bumping beginning.

Many times I want to do something, only to find out it's not as easy as it looks. When I was little and that happened, I often used to give up right then and there. But now I've been around long enough to see a pattern: Almost everything worth trying works that way. If I give up on everything that's hard, heck, I might as well just stay in bed the rest of my life. Bumpy beginnings—bring 'em on!

*H*e doesn't duck the
well-deserved compliment.

—*Arthur Accused!*
by Marc Brown

You already know that it's a good thing to pay compliments to others, to let them know that they've done well or that they look terrific or that they're simply nice. But how good are you on the receiving end of a compliment? Do you accept it gracefully, gratefully? Or do you shrink away in immature awkwardness and flusterment?

**If someone compliments me today, I'll recognize it
for what it is—a gift freely given. I'll face it square-on
and receive it with gratitude.**

Kids throughout this great big world are very much like you.

—*Can You Greet the Whole Wide World?*
12 Common Phrases in 12 Different Languages
by Lezlie Evans
illustrated by Denis Roche

This is true no matter what language kids speak, no matter what flag they pledge allegiance to, no matter their color or their clothes or their unpronounceable names. In many, many ways—and in all ways that really count—they're just like you. Kid Country has no borders. You—and every other kid in the world—became a citizen the day you were born.

Next time I see a kid who appears foreign to me, who looks and speaks strangely, who just plain seems different from me in every way, I'll remember that this is only an illusion. I'll remember that beneath our different appearances lies the common ground of kidhood.

"No time for spats and spouting,"
said the shorthaired calico.

—*Castaway Cats*
by Lisa Wheeler
illustrated by Ponder Goembel

Time and energy. Once you burn a gallon of gas, it's gone forever. Once you burn a minute, you'll never get it back. Use your resources wisely. Don't waste them on petty squabbles and bluster.

There goes another minute. I think I wasted it. Ah, who cares? I've got billions of minutes left . . . don't I?

D o you ever feel
like . . .
you lost your true best friend?
And now you have no one
you can be your dumb self with?

—*Minn and Jake*
by Janet S. Wong
illustrated by Geneviève Côté

It's one thing you'll never outgrow—the need for a friend with whom you can be your own dumb self. It's not good, not healthy, for that dumb self to stay bottled up. It wants to express itself, too, just like your brilliant, public self. This can be done only with someone who makes you totally comfortable. When you find such a person, hang on.

Everybody sees the magnificent, wonderful, brilliant, unmatchable me. But only a few true and trusted friends get to see the goofy, stupid, silly, imperfect, ridiculous me. I wonder if they know what a valuable service they provide. Today I'll say to each of them "Hey, thanks," and when they ask "What for?" I'll just smile and say something dumb.

"Nine times out of ten, talking is a way of avoiding doing things."

—*Dealing with Dragons*
by Patricia C. Wrede

Stop telling your parents, your friends, the whole world what you're going to do. Just do it.

Do I talk too much and do too little? Do I tell everyone what great grades I'm going to get and what great things I'm going to accomplish—and then go play a video game or take a nap? Today I'll make a point of replacing words with action.

The last moments of this championship season. No matter how hard I try to hang on, those moments are already fading as I ride away.

—*Imitate the Tiger*
by Jan Cheripko

When we're in the middle of the best of times, we can't imagine our feelings ever going away. But they do. Even championship seasons fade. Maybe it's nature's way of reminding us to get on with our lives. Life happens forward, into the future. Not backward.

I'll enjoy my championship moments to the fullest. I may even cling to them after they're over—but not too long.

DANCING Matilda DANCES out of bed.

—*Dancing Matilda*
by Sarah Hager
illustrated by Kelly Murphy

OK, enough's enough! I'm trying to be a good sport and follow the daily advice in this book, but there's no way I'm going to get out of bed *dancing*. It's all I can do to pry one eye open. It's all I can do just to roll over enough to fall to the floor, where I resume sleeping until somebody wakes me up again.

On the other hand . . . I do know a couple of Dancing Matildas, kids who seem all bright and perky no matter how early in the morning. I have to admit I'm a little jealous of such kids. I can't help wondering if there's a better way to start the day than the torture I go through. Tell you what—when I wake up tomorrow, I'll do a little dance step on the way to the bathroom and see what happens.

Did you know that Pelé grew up so poor that he had to make his own soccer ball out of a sock stuffed with newspapers?

—*What Athletes Are Made Of*
by Hanoch Piven

And maybe if Pelé had been rich, and maybe if his parents had bought him a brand-new ball every year and up-to-the-minute shoes and a cool headband and wristbands, and maybe if they had driven him to and from practice every day—if Pelé had had all that instead of nothing—maybe he would not have been motivated to become the greatest soccer player of all time.

Is life too easy for me? Do I get almost everything I want? Am I pampered? spoiled? soft? Today I'll run a little test to see if I can make the grade. Instead of taking the usual shortcut, I'll take the long way around. If there's something I look forward to eating every day, I'll go without. I'll ignore my favorite pastime. I'll give myself a taste of the unspoiled life. I will *not* be pampered.

At first Jimmy McGee didn't know he was a hero.

—The Curious Adventures of Jimmy McGee
by Eleanor Estes
illustrated by John O'Brien

A girl steers her friend away from a gaggle of kids—and thereby saves her from overhearing some hateful gossip. A cool, popular kid slaps hands with a mousy, uncool kid—and thereby raises the mouse's status. No medals are given for deeds like these. No bands play. But every day scores of us benefit from the little-noticed, unrewarded acts of unsung heroes.

I walk among unsung heroes. Today I'll try to catch one in the act. And maybe one of these days I'll become an unsung hero myself.

Then she would say, "Please teach me some new words in Spanish."

—*Tomás and the Library Lady*
by Pat Mora
illustrated by Raul Colón

When was the last time you used the words *teach me*? Maybe not since you started first grade? Here's an irony about school: The daily grind of tests, homework, and pressures sometimes blunts rather than stimulates a thirst for knowledge.

Have I lost my thirst for knowledge? Am I less curious now than I used to be? Do I think I already know it all? If the answer to these questions is yes, I'll throw open my bedroom window and call out to the world: "Teach me!"

To me, the labels that people gave each other—or themselves—were like invisible name tags. Once you started to "wear" one, everyone was free to make assumptions about who you are.

—*More Than a Label: Why What You Wear or Who You're with Doesn't Define Who You Are* by Aisha Muharrar

So why do it? Why costume yourself like a this or a that and thereby invite everyone to assume you're so much less than you really are?

I am not a label.
I am not a label.
I am not a label.

"It is always better to be an original than an imitation."

—*Theodore*
by Frank Keating
illustrated by Mike Wimmer

There is one surefire way to be original—be yourself. After all, you are a unique, once-in-a-universe combination of molecules, personality, and experience. To be purely yourself is to be purely original. Is it OK to imitate? Sure . . . sometimes. But don't ignore the uniqueness that is you. Don't deny the world the one-of-a-kind creation that is your own self.

I believe the words above from Teddy Roosevelt.
Today I will do one little thing—a word, a gesture,
whatever—that is pure me, nothing but me, nobody else.
Tomorrow I'll do two.

I smiled and tried to exit gracefully,
and instead I managed to half-trip.

—*Thwonk*
by Joan Bauer

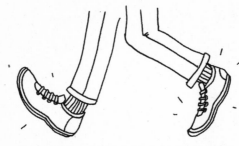

It's no fun being embarrassed. Just when everybody is watching you, you say the wrong thing, do something stupid. You mess up. You stumble and fumble and bumble. You're mortified. You want to lie down and die right there. But take comfort—it's happened to everybody. And the fact is, nobody cares about your bumble nearly as much as you do. So just pick yourself up, dust yourself off, patch up your smile, and carry on. History shows that if you do this—or if you don't—the sun will rise again the next day.

I've made my share of bumbles already, and I'm sure there are more waiting to happen. When they do, I'll just dust myself off and carry on. A bumble can't stick to me if I don't let it.

The fear moved then, moved away, and Brian knew the wolf for what it was—
another part of the woods,
another part of all of it.

—*Hatchet*
by Gary Paulsen

Fear often has to do with feeling apart, separated, different. We humans tend to set the stage for our own fears by separating ourselves from our environment. We separate ourselves from other animals and from other people. One way back from that fear is to close the separation, to view ourselves not so much as creatures apart but as members of the vast family of earth.

No, this doesn't mean I should go running fearlessly and foolishly through the woods looking for bears and wolves to pet. It does mean that I will never knowingly give any animal reason to fear me.

Mr. President, I wish you my good luck in your very hard job. I vote for peace. My grandmother votes with me.

—*Sitti's Secrets*
by Naomi Shihab Nye
illustrated by Nancy Carpenter

Although the subject of the quote above is peace, the subject of this page is communication. Much of the misunderstanding in this world happens because we don't communicate with each other, don't express our thoughts and feelings. Misunderstanding thrives on words unsaid.

Is there something I'm not saying that I should say? If so, today I'll let my thoughts be known to a friend, to a family member—or even to the president.

Come with me. You'll be all right on this Halloweening night.

—*Come with Me on Halloween*
by Linda Hoffman Kimball
illustrated by Mike Reed

If you're going out trick-or-treating, you must do so safely. That means following these three rules:

1. Don't eat your "loot" before showing it to your parents or a responsible adult.

2. Unless you're with an adult, go only to familiar neighborhoods.

3. Don't go alone.

If your parents want to add some other rules, follow them, too.

I'm totally cool with Halloween Safety. If I go out tonight, I will follow the rules above.

I did not mind that Daddy did not call me beautiful, because it took nothing to be beautiful.

—*I Am Morgan le Fay*
by Nancy Springer

It takes nothing to be beautiful. You can't earn it. You can't achieve it. You can't buy it. It's simply an unearned gift. An accident. So why do we make more of a fuss over a beautiful kid than the kid who works his or her butt off to get the highest grade in math class?

Whom do I give my credit to? People who achieve? People who work hard? People who are nice? Or people who just look good?

Being married to the future king was
not all juicy snacks
and squishy pillows.

—*Moi & Marie Antoinette*
by Lynn Cullen
illustrated by Amy Young

Which is not to say that because Marie Antoinette lost her head to the guillotine, the same might happen to you. All we're saying here is that neither money nor circumstance entitles a person to a happy life. For the most part, your life will be the result of what you make of it. Beyond that— hey, good luck to us all!

Not that I wish anything bad for rich or royal people, but it's nice to know that just because I don't happen to have a crown or a castle, I'm not shut out of the Happiness Sweepstakes. My chance to be happy is just as good as anyone else's. And I intend to make the most of it.

Once there was a boy who wanted knowledge.

—*What about Me?*
by Ed Young

That sentence bears repeating: "Once there was a boy who wanted knowledge." Not a bike. Not new sneakers. Not the coolest video game. *Knowledge*. He wanted to know stuff. He wanted to learn. Maybe he knew, or maybe he didn't, that knowledge would carry him further than any bike. And that knowledge would never wear out like sneakers. And that a hundred video games playing all at once are no match for the miracle that happens when knowledge is admitted to a young mind.

I have wanted a lot of things in my lifetime. Many of them have come to me as gifts from others. They have made me happy. But knowledge—that's a gift I must give to myself. It, too, will make me happy. But more than that, it will make me . . . me.

When he was in school he longed
to be out, and when he was out
he longed to be in.

—*The Phantom Tollbooth*
by Norton Juster
illustrated by Jules Feiffer

When we're on the right side, how intensely we appreciate the left! And vice versa. Frustrating, isn't it? But we're stuck with this all-too-human trait, so why not learn from it? There and Then looks really good when viewed from Here and Now. But you know the drill. You know that as soon as you cross over to There and Then, you'll wish you were back in Here and Now. Lesson: As long as you're stuck in Here and Now, you might as well try harder to appreciate it.

Today I will dig my claws of satisfaction deeper
into Here and Now.

No one on this entire planet was
separate from anyone else.
We were all connected.

—*Phoenix Rising*
by Karen Hesse

Put any two people together and sooner or later they'll start drawing lines of separation. I like this; you like that. I won; you lost. We differentiate. We contend. And we forget. We forget that as members of the same species—humans all— we are alike in many more ways than we are different.

Today I'll focus on someone who seems very different from me. Then I'll count five ways in which we're connected.

Wh en it was time to choose teams,
she didn't choose me.

—*The Hating Book*
by Charlotte Zolotow
illustrated by Ben Schecter

The team you didn't get picked for. The part you didn't get. The invitation that never came. Life is an endless audition. The judges include family, friends, enemies, coaches, teachers, admissions departments, nameless committees. Sometimes we get thumbs-up, sometimes thumbs-down. The important thing is not that you never fail but that you profit from your failures, that you understand that you can reach your goal on the other side of the creek by crossing on the stepping-stones of your failures.

Failure is dirt-common. I'll fail plenty today: wrong answers, missed foul shots, non–first place finishes. So I'll stop treating failure as if it were a big deal. Failures aren't roadblocks. They're stepping-stones on the way to where I want to go.

Long ago . . .

—*The Memory Coat*
by Elvira Woodruff
illustrated by Michael Dooling

It is said that kids have no use for the word *then*. It is said that only *now* and *this minute* count with kids. It is said that kids believe time began the day they were born. How sad if this were true. It would mean that kids believe they live on a tiny, isolated island in time. It would mean that when they look back, they fail to see the fascinating human adventure that led up to that day when they were born. It would mean that when they look back, they see . . . nothing.

When I look back, I want to see something. I want to see the people, the events, the human stories that led up to me. Today I'm going to ask the librarian to recommend an interesting nonfiction book about the past. I will not exile myself on an island in time.

I give thanks for things that time nor
circumstance can ever change—
a mother's love, a song. . . .

—*I Am Regina*
by Sally M. Keehn

Promises burn like paper. Yesterday's friend is today's foe.
In a world of change, let's hear it for the things that don't:
your parent's smile, sun sparkle on a dewdrop, apples.
Cherish these things, for they offer a peek into eternity.

Today I will identify one thing that, no matter
what or when, never changes.

"But it didn't occur to them [white scientists] that a black man . . . could be smart enough to calculate the movements of the stars."

—*Dear Benjamin Banneker*
by Andrea Davis Pinkney, illustrated by Brian Pinkney

Stereotype. If this is a new word to you, look it up. Get to know it. Stereotypes are like monsters under the bed—they don't really exist, but that doesn't stop some people from believing in them. "All women hate football." That's a stereotype. Some others: "Real men don't cry." "Rich kids are spoiled." "Jocks are dumb." "Teenagers are rotten." All of these statements—these stereotypes—are false, yet some people act as if they were true. That's the problem with stereotypes: They paint a whole group the same color and thereby unfairly label each individual.

I know how much I would hate to be a victim of stereotyping, but can I honestly say I'm not a stereotype-painter myself? Do I have mistaken beliefs about certain groups of people? Every individual has a right to be judged according to his or her own merits. From now on, I will uphold that right.

"There is plenty, and you are welcome to have some too."

—*Too Many Babas*
by Carolyn Croll

We spend a lot of time getting, buying, collecting, piling up. *Get. Get. Get.* Sometimes it seems that's all we're about—until a little voice whispers: *Share. Share. Share.*

Guilty. I, too, spend a lot of time getting. Stuff for myself, mostly. Today I'll make a point of sharing some of the plenty that I've got. And even if it's not plenty, I'll share, anyway.

It was that regrettable sort of conversation that results from talking with your mouth full.

—*The Wind in the Willows*
by Kenneth Grahame

Table manners. Are they a big deal in your family? If not, check yourself. Do you talk with your mouth full? Snuffle head-down in your food like a starving pig? Wield your fork like a shovel? Ignore your napkin? Reach for the salt over someone's plate? Forget the words *Excuse me* and *Thank you*?

It's time I stopped eating like a little kid. If I want to be taken seriously and respected in the grown-up world, I need to make myself more presentable.
I'll start with table manners.

It isn't walls and furniture that makes a home. It's the family.

—*The Family Under the Bridge*
by Natalie Savage Carlson
illustrated by Garth Williams

A good thought to keep in mind next time your parents decline to buy you everything you want. It is your family, not your possessions, that makes your house a home. There may be a number on your front door, but your true address is written in the hearts of those who say "Sweet dreams" to you each night.

Today I will thank my family for giving me a home.

*H*e'll eat almost anything;
he never picks.

—*Sidney the Silly Who Only Eats 6*
by M. W. Penn
illustrated by Sarah Tommer

Kids are famous for being picky eaters: unwilling to try something new, no sense of adventure. A worldful of cool flavors goes untasted because nothing scares a picky eater more than biting into something he or she hasn't already eaten a million times before. The gastronomic life of a picky eater can be described in one word: *bor-ing!*

Is my gastronomic life a dull, boring thud? Am I missing out on a wonderful world of flavors? Today I'll stop being a big baby long enough to try something new.

He tidied up after himself.

—*Too Many Frogs!*
by Sandy Asher
illustrated by Keith Graves

Do you leave the cap off the toothpaste? the toilet unflushed? Do you hang up your jacket or just toss it wherever? Does it ever occur to you to turn off a light, return the sofa cushion to its place, put your dirty dishes in the sink or dishwasher? Do you walk away from spills because that's what parents are for, to clean up their kids' messes . . . right?

Wrong.
My parents are not my servants. This is their house as well as mine, so what right do I have to make them live in my mess? And I'm pretty sure there's no law saying Every Kid Who Is Not a Slob Will Be Thrown in Jail.
Starting today, I will clean up after myself.

In dismay each discovered that the more arrows they acquired, the more terrified they became.

—Feathers and Fools
by Mem Fox
illustrated by Nicholas Wilton

Weapons—be they guns and arrows or gossip and lies—never seem to bring peace to those who use them. Instead of settling things and bringing comfort, they lead to more weapons, and more, until everyone is armed and afraid.

I've seen the damage that gossip and lies can do, both to the people who wield them and to their targets. I do not need such weapons to get through the day. I will do my best to neither attack nor counterattack. I shall walk unarmed.

Though Nessa disliked this chore,
she found herself smiling.

—*Prairie River: Journey of Faith*
by Kristiana Gregory

The point is this: Nessa is not smiling *because of* her chore; she's smiling *in spite of* it. Nobody expects you to *enjoy* your chores. It's unfair to compare chores to fun. Chores are chores. Chores are work. And so is much of life—doing things not because they're fun but because they're necessary.

I'm glad to have this new view of my chores. Next time I'm washing the dishes or taking out the trash, I'll just accept it for what it is: work that has to be done. No big deal. Just the way life is. Hey, since I won't be complaining, maybe I'll even find a reason to smile!

U nfortunately, not all websites
are run by honest people.

—Internet Safety
by Josepha Sherman

"Don't believe everything you read or hear." That old warning originally referred to newspapers and radio. Now it applies equally to the Internet. In some ways the Internet is like the Old West—anything goes. Meaning you've got to be your own sheriff.

I hear you. I'll be Internet-careful.

If you cannot dance, you will say,
"The drumming is poor."
—Ashanti

—The Night Has Ears: African Proverbs
by Ashley Bryan

"I woulda won the race, but the others started too soon."

"I woulda got an A, but the teacher stinks."

"I could read that book in ten minutes—I just don't feel like it."

Reasons, reasons. We love to give reasons for our shortcomings. Like, if all those reasons would just disappear, we would suddenly be revealed as the Most Magnificent and Perfect Creature in the History of the Universe. Too bad we spend so much time making excuses for what we *can't* do instead of spending that priceless time tracking down and perfecting what we *can* do.

I already have an idea what I'm good at and what I'm not good at. Today I'll try to find a new thing that I'm good at.
As for the not-good stuff—no excuses.
Because nobody's perfect, not even me.

"Maybe I've said too much."

—*Brown Sunshine of Sawdust Valley*
by Marguerite Henry
illustrated by Bonnie Shields

blah, blah, blah blah, blah...

Did it ever occur to you that maybe it's a shame that talk comes so easily for most of us? We learn to talk as toddlers and—bam!—we're off to a lifetime of yapping. How much better might human communication be if words were as precious as diamonds? If each of us were allotted only 100 words per day?

Consider this: When President Lincoln gave his Gettysburg Address, he wasn't even the main speaker that day. That honor went to the famous orator Edward Everett. Everett's speech, which contained 13,607 words, lasted for two hours. Lincoln spoke next—for two minutes. Nearly a century and a half later, kids memorize every one of his 272 words. Nobody remembers what Everett said.

Today I will begin saying more with less.

I wash my hands.

—*Hurry Up!*
by Carol Murray
illustrated by Dave Garbot

You turn a doorknob and enter a room. You don't even think about it. Nor do you think about the herd of germs that moves from the doorknob to your hand. Fifteen minutes later you're eating a sandwich. The germs have now moved from your hand to the sandwich, from the sandwich to your mouth, and now they're in your stomach, soon to be in your bloodstream. The good news is that such germs are usually harmless—usually, but not always. Sometimes, in this manner, a doorknob—or a textbook or a comb or a handshake or any of a thousand other "harmless" things—can make you sick. Unless you interrupt the germ-hopping process by . . . *washing your hands.*

Today I will either continue or begin a good, healthy habit:
I will wash my hands before I leave a lavatory
and before I eat.

Way to go, Sam!

—*Fix It, Sam*
by Lori Ries
illustrated by Sue Ramá

Congratulations are fun to receive. You can never get too many, right? But how about *giving* congratulations? Like gifts, congratulations make the giver as well as the receiver feel good. But let's take it a step further. Everyone congratulates the kid who wins the big game or makes a perfect score on a test. But how about the kid who really has to struggle to get a B—and does it? Or the kid who sits on the bench on game day—but helps the first-stringers get better on practice days? Or the kid whose clarinet you never hear because it blends so well with the music of the band? Who will congratulate them?

I will.

I have heard of a land
Where the imagination has no fences
Where what is dreamed one night
Is accomplished the next day

—*I Have Heard of a Land*
by Joyce Carol Thomas
illustrated by Floyd Cooper

Sound impossible? It really happened, in the 1880s. The land was the Oklahoma Territory. At the crack of a pistol, thousands of homesteaders raced their horses and wagons across the prairie flats to claim for themselves a piece of the American Dream.

I live in a magical land, a land where imagination meets possibility, a land that says "Tell me your dream, kid." Today I'll do just that. I'll find a quiet spot and whisper my dream—just between America and me.

The Pilgrims . . . spoke the same
language, wore the same clothes, and
worshiped the same way. They had
no diversity until they met
the Native Americans.

—*P Is for Pilgrim: A Thanksgiving Alphabet*
by Carol Crane
illustrated by Helle Urban

Unless you're a Native American, your ancestors were not the first to live on this land. From the Atlantic to the Pacific, there was a culture of custom and poetry and stewardship of the earth that compels our attention today.

"Cowboys and Indians" were OK for little-kid comic books, but now I'd like to find out more about the Native Americans who flourished here long before the Pilgrims arrived. Today I'll check out a book at the library.

There was something special about this Joplin music.

—*Raggin': A Story About Scott Joplin*
by Barbara Mitchell
illustrated by Hetty Mitchell

If you were born a hundred years ago, you'd probably think Scott Joplin's music was as cool as you think your own favorite music is today. *News flash:* Lots of good stuff happened before you were ever born. Don't cheat yourself by ignoring everything that's older than you. That goes for music.

Today I'll ask my parents about their favorite music.
Tomorrow I'll ask my grandparents.

"We can't take any credit for our talents.
It's how we use them that counts."

—*A Wrinkle in Time*
by Madeleine L'Engle

If you were born extraflexible and astound your friends by bending your thumb all the way back to your wrist—well, that's nice, but don't go giving yourself a trophy. You didn't earn a thing. On the other hand, if you were blessed with a good voice and you belong to a singing group that recently entertained the folks at a retirement home—then go ahead, give yourself a little credit. You're making good use of your talent.

Somewhere inside me is a talent that so far seems hidden from everyone, including me. Today I'm going to start tracking down that talent, and when I find it, I'll put it to good use.

I admire Mom, even when she's mad at me, and I know she loves me.

—*Strider*
by Beverly Cleary
illustrated by Paul O. Zelinsky

It's OK to have family disagreements. It's OK for parents and kids to be mad at each other. And it's OK to say so. Why? Because a strong relationship is an honest relationship, and no honest relationship is all peaches and cream. Love is the key. Where love abides, anger is but a passing visitor.

My parents love me. I tend to forget this
when I fight with them.
Repeat: My parents love me.

The letters tried to think of something important, *really* important. Finally they knew what to say. What could be more important than peace?

—*The Alphabet Tree*
by Leo Lionni

Peace isn't just for world-famous big shots—presidents, prime ministers, Nobel Prize winners. You can play a role, too, in your school, your community. The best place to begin is right in your own home. Learn to wage peace, not war, in your kitchen, your living room, your backyard.

Why should I expect nations to harmonize if I can't even get along with my brother or sister or parents? Today I'll do one small thing to keep the peace at home.

Then he kicked the stump
from underneath Alvin,
snapping the man's neck instantly.

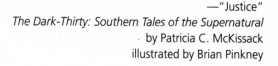

—"Justice"
The Dark-Thirty: Southern Tales of the Supernatural
by Patricia C. McKissack
illustrated by Brian Pinkney

The story is fiction. Alvin is fiction. But the fate he suffers in the story was all too real for many people. They, like Alvin, were lynched because other people didn't like the color of their skin. Oh, that was the old days, you say. Things like that could never happen again.

You sure?

This will be Alvin Day. Even though he's fictional, he represents real people, real victims of racism, so that's how I'll think of him. Throughout the day, I will remember this man who was hanged because of his color. I will not allow myself to forget him. And in so doing, I will be joining the fight against hate crimes.

*H*er naʻau, gut feeling, pressed her
to keep walking.

—*The Sleeping Giant:*
A Tale from Kauaʻi
retold and illustrated by Edna Cabcabin Moran

Your brain isn't your only source of information. Some-times it's your gut, or wherever it is that "gut feelings" re-side. Gut feelings don't "think." They're just there, under your skin, ready to steer you this way or that when you've a choice to make. They're not guaranteed to be right, but often they are.

I may not always follow my gut feeling—my *naʻau*—
but I will always, always listen to it.

As for her temper, it improved as well. Her mouth could still get terrible fierce at times, but she would whisper to herself, "Loving heart, loving heart."

—*The Wishing of Biddy Malone*
by Joy Cowley
illustrated by Christopher Denise

You've heard of ghost whisperers and horse whisperers? Well, there are temper whisperers, too—and one of them is *you*. For nothing cools off a temper better than a word from the temper's owner—a word so soft that the temper must quiet down in order to hear it.

The next time I feel my temper rising, I will do like Biddy Malone: I'll whisper a loving word in its ear.

The holiday is all about light,
a gathering of light, and we put our
menorah in the parlor window
so passersby can see.

—*Dreams in the Golden Country: The Diary of Zipporah Feldman,
a Jewish Immigrant Girl, New York City, 1903*
(Dear America series)
by Kathryn Lasky

"So passersby can see." What a nice and telling way to exercise the freedom of religion that is a cornerstone of the American Experiment. In other times and other places, you might have had to hide your menorah or cross or any other sign that you practiced a forbidden religion. Every time you decline to cast a stone at a religion you don't personally believe in, you confirm the success of the Experiment.

I can't deny that I have a hard time relating to some religions. But that's OK. It's only natural. The important thing is that I support other people's right to believe what they want to believe.

Most entertainment today focuses around buying or paying for something (tickets to a concert, a DVD rental, shopping with friends).

—*All Made Up: A Girl's Guide to Seeing Through Celebrity Hype . . . and Celebrating Real Beauty*
by Audrey D. Brashich
illustrated by Shawn Banner

Do fun and money go hand in hand for you? Could you survive for a day, a week, without money? Like to try?

OK, I'll take the challenge. The next time I get my allowance or some gift money, I'll put it in a drawer and design a Day without Money. I'll resolve not merely to survive it but to maybe even enjoy it.

"I know who I am."

—*Dancing through the Snow*
by Jean Little

These words are spoken by Min, a foundling with no mother, no birth certificate, no baby pictures. And so she creates her own identity, day by day, through the loving actions of a life well lived.

Do I know who I am? Truly? Sure, I know my name and where I was born and how old I am and my favorite color and my favorite flavor of ice cream. But do I really know the answer to the question *Who am I?* Today I'll take a blank sheet of paper and in fifty words or less try to answer the question—honestly. Then, if I care to, I'll answer it once a year from now on.

"Well, look at the bright side," said Fred. "If you're dead, you won't have to go to school Monday."

—*The Not-So-Jolly Roger*
(The Time Warp Trio)
by Jon Scieszka
illustrated by Lane Smith

OK, it's a little extreme, but you get the point: Having to go to school is *not* the worst thing in the world.

Hey, there are worse things than going to school.
Like being trapped in a clothes dryer with a thousand spiders. But, seriously, let's look at the good side: I don't have to go out and make a living; I get to be with friends all day; I get to learn stuff; I have this incredible smorgasbord of activities to choose from; I get to express myself in a million ways, like I won't be able to do when I grow up and have to narrow myself down to a single, make-a-living job.
(Which doesn't mean I can't still love snow days.)
Today I will not dread school.

UNLESS someone like you
cares a whole awful lot,
nothing is going to get better.
It's not.

—*The Lorax*
by Dr. Seuss

When bad things turn good, the reason can usually be found in the human heart—sometimes in the hearts of great masses of people, sometimes in the heart of a solitary soul.

Today I will identify just one thing that I care about, one thing that's not doing so good. Then I'll ask myself this question: How can I make it better?

Papa always said you make
your own luck.

—*Boston Jane: An Adventure*
by Jennifer L. Holm

Sure, there are exceptions. Why should one lucky bloke win the lottery over ten million equally deserving blokes? But pay attention to the good things that happen to people around you, and if you bring in the honesty and lock out the jealousy, you may notice a curious thing: Good luck has a way of falling on those who work hardest.

This is great news! It means I'm not totally at the mercy of capricious forces. It means that, with my own efforts, I can increase the chances that I'll get lucky.

Rrrrrriiiiinnnnnggggg . . . WHACK!
Shhhh, alarm clock.

—*Hey, Pancakes!*
by Tamson Weston
illustrated by Stephen Gammell

Do your mother and father have to call you forty-seven times to get up in the morning? Do they have to toot tubas and beat drums? Do they have to tip the bed up at one end and send you sliding onto the floor?

OK, OK, I get the point. If I haven't done so already, as of tomorrow I will cease using my parents as Mr. and Mrs. Alarm Clock. I will get a real alarm clock, and when it sounds off in the morning, I will shock the world—I will get out of bed. *All by myself.*

It's a funny thing about parents. You think you know them pretty well and then one day they let something slip and you see them in a brand-new light.

—*Orwell's Luck*
by Richard Jennings

When we're little kids, we think we own our parents. We can't imagine them without us. It's as if we invented them. And then one day we find out that they're not just parents—they're *people*!—with histories and lives all their own. This new knowledge may feel uncomfortable at first, even unwelcome. But pretty soon you'll see it as a good thing, because discovering that your parents are people is a sign that you're growing up—and that they are soon to become your friends in a way that could never have happened when you owned them.

Have I yet come to see my parents as people? If not, I look forward to that day, when I will embark on a new relationship with them.

What I have since realized is that if people expect you to be brave, sometimes you pretend that you are.

—*Walk Two Moons*
by Sharon Creech

And, we might add, the longer you pretend, the more likely you are to become whatever you are pretending to be. Sometimes virtue comes from other people. It is society's way of improving its membership. Do others seem to expect too much of you? Do you cringe to think what people would say if only they knew the *real* you? If so, note this: Your potential is probably more visible to others than to you.

If other people seem to have a higher opinion of me than I have of myself, I'll trust them. I'll use their opinion as a stepping-stone up to my potential. And if I feel as if I'm faking it, I'll remember that *pretend* is just another word for *practice.*

But every time Mr. Mallard saw what looked like a nice place, Mrs. Mallard said it was no good.

—*Make Way for Ducklings*
by Robert McCloskey

Maybe Mrs. Mallard has her reasons, but let's face it—people who shoot down everybody else's suggestions are hard to take.

Am I hard to take? Do I welcome other people's suggestions, or does it have to be my way or no way? I'll monitor myself today and find out.

So Rose did her best to greet
each of the guests.
"How do you do?" "Nice to
meet you too!"

—*While Mama Had a Quick Little Chat*
by Amy Reichert
illustrated by Alexandra Boiger

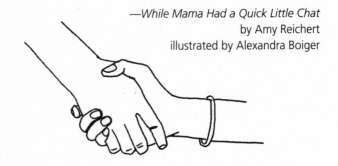

You're not a little kid anymore. A simple thing like greeting your parents' friends on the street or in the living room is a terrific proving ground for the grown-up social life that lies ahead.

If I meet friends of my parents today, even if they're strangers to me, I won't run or stare at my shoes like an immature little kid. I'll look them in the eye and shake their hands and say "Nice to meet you, too."

And *everybody* wanted a suit like his.

—*Halibut Jackson*
by David Lucas

Here's all that needs to be said: Do *you* want to be everybody?

No, I don't want to be everybody. I want to be me.

"Sometimes," he said, "when you lose a gift, you get another one."

—*Up Close: Johnny Cash*
by Anne E. Neimark

And that's not so surprising, is it? A gift, by definition, is not something you earn or even deserve—it's something given to you. It happens to you, and it can just as easily un-happen to you. And just as easily be replaced by yet another gift, which at first you may not even recognize as such.

I, like everyone, was born with gifts. Others have happened to me along the way. Some gifts may stay with me for a lifetime; some have already gone. So it is with gifts: They come and go. I will remember this and not feel so bad next time a gift un-happens to me.

*H*old fast to your dream, Sarah.
Wrap it.

—*Donuthead*
by Sue Stauffacher

Why do we wrap things? Usually to protect them. The more fragile they are, the more important the wrapping. Your dream is prey to many perils. It may shatter under the blows of criticism, evaporate with competition's heat, sink to the bottomless depths of others' indifference. Tend to your dream. Protect it as you would a fallen nestling. Until the day when it—and you—will fly.

Is my dream in danger? Today I will wrap it in determination and confidence. *My* dream will survive.

Never walk on ice unless it has been officially declared safe.

—*A Kid's Winter EcoJournal*
by Toni Albert
illustrated by Margaret Brandt

Every year people drown because they fall through thin ice. The problem with thin ice is that it doesn't look any different from ice a hundred feet thick. So that's why you do the sensible thing, the intelligent thing: You stay away unless some authority tells you it's safe. And for those of you in Florida, where the only ice is in your fridge: Don't jump into a swimming pool before checking for alligators.

If I come upon ice covering a pond or stream, I won't trust it. My life isn't worth the risk.

"My gift is obedience. Ella will always be obedient."

—*Ella Enchanted*
by Gail Carson Levine

Gift? How about curse? Even the strictest parent wouldn't wish total, lifetime obedience on a child. Should you obey when a neighbor says "Smoke this cigarette"? When a classmate says "Let me copy your answers"? When a friend says "Don't tell your parents"? Obedience isn't just about following orders. It's also about knowing *whose* orders to follow.

Once upon a time, all rules came from my parents. As I get older, I notice that the circle of command grows to include teachers, neighbors, coaches, instructors, lifeguards, police officers, etc. My job now is not to obey everyone but to figure out *whom* I trust enough to obey.

"*O*h," she sighed. . . . "I would like very much to be *famous.*"

—*Veronica*
by Roger Duvoisin

There's a lot of fame going around these days.

"I'm famous."

"Really? What for?"

"Oh, nothing. I'm just famous."

"Cool!"

It's not a crime to wish for fame. But keep in mind this old saying: "Be careful what you wish for—you might get it." Fame without achievement is empty and, in the end, unsatisfying.

I'll set my sights on achievement, not fame. If fame comes along for the ride, fine, but I'll keep it in the backseat.

What bothered me was not knowing why I'd done it. A lie is the opposite of the truth. Truth is good and lies are bad. Black and white. Simple. Still, I'd lied to Alice for no good reason, and I hadn't even felt bad about it until I'd gotten caught.

—*So B. It*
by Sarah Weeks

Look at this mess: (1) The narrator tells a lie; (2) she doesn't know why she lied; (3) it bugs her that she doesn't know why; (4) she finally feels bad; (5) but only *after* she's caught. Lying complicates your life, twists it and tangles it till you're nothing but knots.

I will try to go through this whole day without telling a lie (unless maybe it's a small, helpful one—see July 25). When I lay my head down tonight, there will be no knots in my string.

But I'd rather have Mama than money.

—*Home for Navidad*
by Harriet Ziefert
illustrated by Santiago Cohen

So you're thinking, Well, *duh,* of course I'd rather have my mother than money. I mean, *if* I *had* to choose between the two. I mean, like, *if* I absolutely could not have both at the same time. But, hey, if I could, like, have Mom on Monday *and* money on Tuesday, I mean, y'know, switch off every other day? . . . And when she saw the great clothes and stuff I bought on my money days, well, she'd be *happy* for me, right? . . . And, anyway, I can be such a pain, she'd probably be *glad* to get rid of me half the time. . . .

I'll leave all the weaseling to the paragraph above and say simply, today, to my mother, "Mom, I'd rather have you than money." And give her a kiss. And then do the same for Dad.

There is nothing in the world so irresistibly contagious as laughter and good humor.

—*A Christmas Carol*
by Charles Dickens

If Ebenezer Scrooge could not resist good cheer, who can? What a wonderful pandemic that would be—good humor leaping from continent to continent, infecting everyone it touched, sweeping the globe like a fabulous flu.

I've heard of people in India who meet before work every day and do group belly laughing instead of calisthenics. Maybe they're onto something. And maybe I've been holding back. Today I'll make a point of laughing out loud at least once. If during a whole day I can't find one thing to laugh out loud about—well, Scrooge on me.

"I need a hug tonight," Ruby told Miss Arbutus before going to her room.

—*Way Down Deep*
by Ruth White

Notice that Ruby doesn't say she *wants* a hug; she says she *needs* it. You're probably an expert at knowing what you want, but how good are you at knowing what you need? To truly know what you need, you must know yourself more honestly and completely than you know anyone else.

There are things that I need—not want, but need. Things without which I may never reach my potential. First I must identify myself, know myself, understand myself. Then my needs will present themselves.

The two times he found a wallet, he took them to the lost-and-found departments of local stores.

—*True Talents*
by David Lubar

A wallet, a cell phone, an iPod, a bracelet—what happens when you come across something like this and no one is around? Do you turn it over to the lost and found or some responsible person? Or do you listen to the little gremlin who whispers "Finders keepers" and stick it in your pocket?

If I find something that obviously belongs to someone else, I'll do the right thing—because I know that if I were the one who lost it, I'd hope the person finding it would ignore the whispering gremlin.

I used to make snow angels . . . to cheer up our neighbor, Mrs. Conoway, who lived alone.

—*The Trial*
by Jen Bryant

Cheering up a lonely neighbor—now, that's a day well spent. It doesn't cost a dime, and the payoff is a warm smile. And don't forget the bonus: You have fun doing it. Look around—there are Mrs. Conoways everywhere.

Today I will make a neighbor smile.

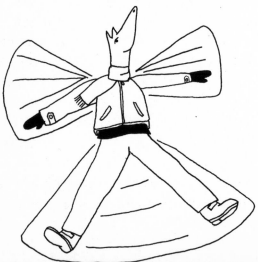

*H*e opened a bank account.

—*Rock, Brock, and the Savings Shock*
by Sheila Bair
illustrated by Barry Gott

Are you waiting to grow up? Do you figure it will happen overnight? Like, you'll wake up one morning in your twenties or whenever, and—poof!—you'll be a grown-up. This kind of thinking gives you an excuse to put off your maturity and continue your irresponsible, little-kid ways long after you've stopped growing. The fact is, growing up takes place over a span of years, in hundreds, even thousands, of little steps. One of those steps is getting and learning to use your own bank account.

If I have more than $5 lying around and don't already have my own bank account, I'll ask my parents about getting one.

"Hey! Unto you a child is born!"

—*The Best Christmas Pageant Ever*
by Barbara Robinson

When rascally Gladys Herdman belts out the only speaking part in the play, she turns the traditional Christmas story on its ear—and in so doing makes it more meaningful than ever to the people in the audience. Profane, troublemaking, cigar-chomping Gladys Herdman bellows on behalf of misfits everywhere: "Hey! Maybe ya don't like us! But don't ignore us! Listen to us! Ya might learn somethin'!"

Do I know any out-of-step Gladys Herdmans? Have I ignored them? Looked down my nose at them? Maybe they have a new spin on things that I haven't considered. Maybe they're saying something I'd like to hear— if only I would listen. Today I will.

Now let me tell you
what the Muslims believe.

—*Tales of Persia: Missionary Stories from Islamic Iran*
by William McElwee Miller
illustrated by Bruce Van Patter

Don't rely on headlines and TV news snippets to inform you about the world you live in. Go beyond the headlines. Read the whole story. Read a book. View a documentary. Attend a lecture. Talk with others. Don't let headlines determine your beliefs. Gather the facts, then decide for yourself what to believe.

What do I actually know about Muslims? Are they all
alike? Do they all eat the same food? Laugh at the same
things? Or are they as varied as my neighbors?
Today I'll start to find out more about these people
who share my planet and my country.

*"The moral of the panda fable is this:
Sometimes what you already have
is the best thing."*

—*Gooney the Fabulous*
by Lois Lowry
illustrated by Middy Thomas

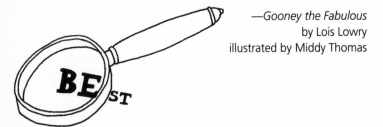

Why does value seem to depend on distance? We barely pay attention to something right in front of our nose, while something half as worthy we covet because it's a thousand miles away. The closer things are, the less we see them. It doesn't make sense, does it? Curious to know what best things you may be overlooking?

Do I spend too much time wishing I had better this, better that? Maybe I already have the best but I just don't know it. Today I'll make a list I'll call My Ten Least Things: ten components of my life—things, people, places—that I notice the least and that I can least do without.

"Oh, beautiful day, it is here at last!"

—*Charlotte's Web*
by E. B. White

Wilbur—now, there's a pig who knows how to wake up. Not with a slump and a grump but with a bright greeting for a promising day. While it's true that we cannot always know what a day will hold for us, it's also true that the day often conforms to the shape of our outlook.

I understand that, in spite of all the people who may say "Have a great day" to me, this day may turn out to be a bummer. On the other hand, I also understand that I can give it a push in the right direction by greeting this new day with an optimistic outlook.

"The first real snow of the year! I've been waiting all winter for this."

—*The Boy from the Basement*
by Susan Shaw

Expectation. It keeps us going. The first snow. The first kiss. The first job. What would life be like without something to look forward to?

If I slump into a blah minute today, or a blah half hour, I will think of something I'm looking forward to and say "bye-bye" to the blah.

On a clear, moonless night, you can often see a hazy band of pale light stretching across the sky.

—*Galaxies*
by Seymour Simon

That hazy band of pale light is the Milky Way. Though it won't appear on the mail that comes to your house, it's part of your address. It's your cosmic neighborhood.

If I can't see the Milky Way because of light pollution where I live, I'll find out where the night sky is dark and the stars are many. I'll go there some clear, moonless night and experience the thrill of seeing my ultimate neighborhood.

"'Tis a good life."

—*The Witch of Blackbird Pond*
by Elizabeth George Speare

Well, here we are, on the last page of the book—and the first page of the rest of your life. We hope the preceding pages have helped guide you through your days. This book does not deny that life can be uncomfortable at best, rotten and tragic at worst. What it tries most to do is to remind you that you are not without resources that can help you cope, and that perhaps the most precious resource of all is your own attitude. If you look for the good things in life, you will find them. If you believe that, in spite of its problems and bad times, life is basically good—it will be.

I understand that some things are beyond my control. I also understand that my view of life depends on choices I make. I hereby choose to view the cookie as half remaining rather than half gone. When life challenges me, I shall turn to my resources: the healing love of friends when I am hurt, the promise of new opportunity when I am rejected, my own common sense when I am afraid, confidence in myself when I am alone. I hereby choose to believe that life is good.

ACKNOWLEDGMENT

Especially helpful in our research was *Quotations for Kids*, compiled and edited by J. A. Senn and published by Millbrook Press.

Eileen Spinelli is the author of almost fifty books for young readers, including *Princess Pig,* illustrated by Tim Bowers, and *Summerhouse Time* for Knopf, as well as picture books such as *Night Shift Daddy,* illustrated by Melissa Iwai, and *I Like Noisy, Mom Likes Quiet,* illustrated by Lydia Halverson.

Jerry Spinelli is the author of many books for young readers, including *Stargirl; Love, Stargirl; Milkweed; Eggs; Smiles to Go; Maniac Magee,* winner of the Newbery Medal; *Wringer,* a Newbery Honor Book; *Crash;* and *Knots in My Yo-yo String,* his autobiography.

Jerry and Eileen are married and live in eastern Pennsylvania. You can learn more about them at www.eileenspinelli.com, www.jerryspinelli.com, and www.randomhouse.com/features/jerryspinelli.